THE LOST WRECK
of the
ISIS

First published in the United States by
Scholastic Inc.,
730 Broadway, New York, N.Y. 10003

Library of Congress Cataloging-in-Publication Data
Ballard, Robert D.
  The Lost Wreck of the Isis/by Robert D. Ballard.
  p. cm. — (A Time quest book)
  Summary: Dr. Ballard visits the Mediterranean to
explore a Roman shipwreck site and investigate an active
underwater volcano.
ISBN 0-590-43852-2 $15.95 (Scholastic Hardcover)
ISBN 0-590-43853-0 $6.95 (Scholastic Paperback)
  1. Sicily (Italy)–Antiquities. Roman–Juvenile literature.
2. Shipwrecks–Italy–Sicily–Juvenile literature.
3. Underwater archaeology–Italy–Sicily–Juvenile literature.
4. Romans–Italy–Sicily–Juvenile literature.
[1. Sicily (Italy)–Antiquities. Roman.   2. Shipwrecks
3. Underwater archaeology   4. Archaeology
5. Romans–Italy–Sicily.]
I. Title.   II. Series.
DG55.S5B35   1990
930.1'028'04091638–dc20   89–70280   CIP   AC

DESIGN AND ART DIRECTION: Pronk&Associates Inc.

ILLUSTRATION: Wesley Lowe, Ken Marschall

EDITORIAL: Hugh Brewster, Nan Froman, Shelley Tanaka

PRODUCTION: Susan Barrable, Donna Chong

PRINTER: Khai Wah Litho Pte Ltd.

(Previous page) A Roman wall painting depicting slaves
carrying sacks of grain on board a river boat.

(Right) Robert Ballard and his team at work on their
underwater robot, JASON.

Produced by

Madison Press Books
40 Madison Avenue
Toronto, Ontario
Canada M5R 2S1
Printed in Singapore

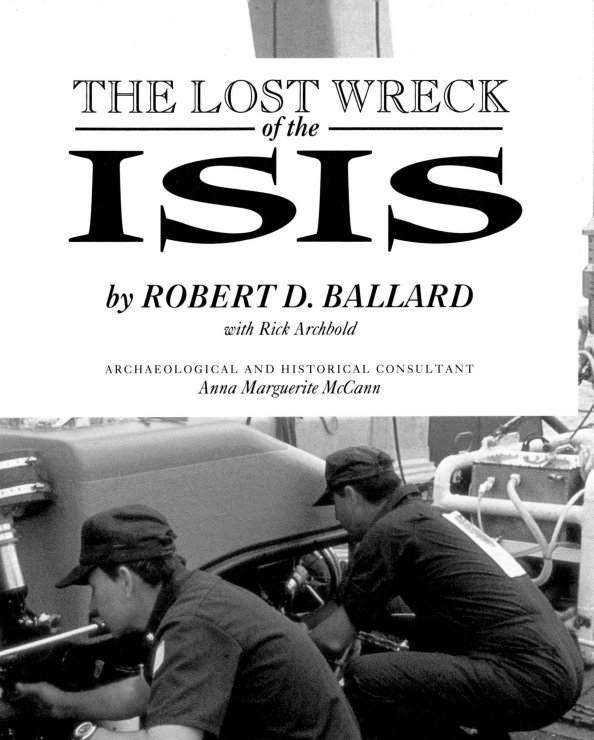

THE LOST WRECK
of the
ISIS

by ROBERT D. BALLARD

with Rick Archbold

ARCHAEOLOGICAL AND HISTORICAL CONSULTANT
Anna Marguerite McCann

A Scholastic/Madison Press Book

*To my first son, Todd Alan Ballard, who was at my side
when we discovered the Roman sailing ship,* Isis, *and the German
battleship,* Bismarck, *and who died tragically one month later.
He was the best flyer of* Argo *I have ever had, and I am going to
miss him on our future voyages of discovery.
And to his caring mother, Marjorie, and proud brother,
Douglas, who love and miss him as much as I do.*

Contents

TWO THOUSAND YEARS AGO the mighty Roman Empire controlled the Mediterranean Sea. From Rome's seaport town of Ostia, hundreds of ships regularly set sail for foreign ports. Many ships completed voyage after voyage safely, and the merchants who owned them became richer and richer. But sometimes sudden storms with enormous waves and raging winds would batter a ship apart, drowning everyone on board and scattering wreckage and cargo over the sea floor.

ROBERT BALLARD AND HIS TEAM fell silent as JASON, their high-tech underwater robot approached the ancient shipwreck. JASON's controller moved his joystick and the robot, half a mile below, turned and shone his lights downwards. There, in the darkness on the sea floor, lay the remains of a Roman ship, unseen for over sixteen centuries. Could JASON's mechanical arms scoop up some of the ancient objects and bring them to the surface? If so, the JASON Project would be a giant step forward in the exploration of the dark, unknown world of the deep ocean.

CHAPTER ONE

Discovery · 1988

"Bob, Bob, wake up!" It was pitch-dark and somebody was pounding on the door of my cabin.

"What is it?" I answered groggily.

"Stromboli," came the muffled reply. "The captain said you wanted to see Stromboli."

"Oh, thanks, yeah, I'll be right up," I mumbled, only half understanding the message.

Then I remembered. I had asked to be wakened when we passed the volcanic island of Stromboli. Known as the lighthouse of the Mediterranean, Stromboli's fiery eruptions had guided sailors crossing the sea for centuries.

I turned over in the narrow bunk and fumbled for my watch. Its luminous green dial said two a.m. I debated whether to get up. I was dog-tired. Long hours at sea and the stress of our frustrating undersea search had taken their toll. But I knew this might be the only chance I'd have to see Stromboli by night.

Our research ship, the *Starella*, on the Mediterranean Sea in June of 1988.

I switched on the light, pulled on some jeans and a shirt, slid my bare feet into shoes and headed for the deck. Topside the air was warm and there was no wind or noise — a beautiful June night on the Mediterranean. The sea was so calm it looked like a black mirror as it reflected the lights of our ship. And there, just ahead on the horizon, was Stromboli, a huge dark cone rising silently out of the sea. Perched over the volcano's left shoulder was a glowing full moon. It looked so close I imagined I could see the car tracks the astronauts had left on its dusty surface.

It was too much to hope that the lighthouse-keeper would wake up and turn on the light, I thought to myself. As if in answer, the volcano suddenly began to erupt, red trickles of lava appearing at its black peak. It wasn't violent like the famous eruption of Vesuvius that had buried the city of Pompeii in A.D. 79. Stromboli was just bubbling over, doing what scientists call "fountaining."

Soon my son Todd, Betsey Robinson and other members of the JASON team had gathered on deck. Todd was in his last year of high school and Betsey was in her third year at Harvard, where she was studying archaeology. Both had summer jobs as part of our team. Then the film crew from National Geographic Television came up on deck and began setting up to videotape the scene. But the rest of us were quiet, staring at the volcano. It was like being present at the birth of our planet. There was nothing human there, just this mighty demonstration of the earth's power. While the eruption continued, our ship, the *Starella*, drew closer, as if drawn by a magnet across the glassy sea. We came within a mile of the island, leaving it to starboard as we headed south for

(**Above**) A close-up photograph of Stromboli erupting.

(**Inset**) Gazing out at Stromboli from the deck of the *Starella*, I ponder the many challenges facing us in our quest for an ancient shipwreck.

the Strait of Messina, the narrow channel that separates Sicily and the toe of Italy.

The next morning, our team of explorers would resume the search for an ancient shipwreck as the first phase of the JASON Project continued. Already we'd been searching for more than a week, and our goal seemed as far away as the golden fleece sought by the original Jason in the days of ancient Greece. Our modern-day JASON was a state-of-the-art underwater robot equipped with cameras that would enable us to explore the ocean floor by remote control instead of using dangerous and inefficient manned submarines. But at this point JASON was still being built; this year we were conducting our search with *Argo*, the same deep-towed vehicle whose video cameras had found the wreck of the *Titanic*.

Jason and the Golden Fleece

Our underwater robot and our Mediterranean expedition were named after the legendary explorer, Jason. Jason's uncle promised to make him king if he captured the golden fleece which had once belonged to a beautiful golden ram. Jason bravely set off in a ship called the *Argo* with his warriors in search of the fleece. During their long voyage they had many brushes with death and disaster. But the gods and goddesses caused a princess, Medea, to fall in love with Jason and use her magic powers to help him. The Greek vase (**above**) shows the goddess Athena protecting Jason as he reaches for the fleece.

Volcanoes in the Mediterranean

The volcanic activity in this part of the Mediterranean is mainly the result of a collision between two pieces of the earth's crust, known as plates. The theory that describes the movement of the crust is known as plate tectonics. When plates collide, the heavier plate is pushed down under the edge of the lighter plate, where some of it melts and becomes magma, or liquid rock. This magma is the lava that you see during a volcanic eruption.

We now know that the continents and the ocean floors are in constant motion and that the whole crust of the earth is divided into plates about 60 miles (100 kilometres) thick. Hundreds of millions of years ago, the earth's land mass was one huge continent that cracked into pieces and drifted apart. That's why, if you look at a map of the globe, you can imagine

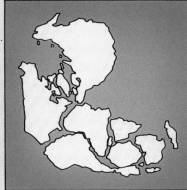

The earth's continents as they appeared 300 million years ago.

Fifty million years ago, the continents have drifted further apart.

Next spring, in the second phase of the project, our plan was to return to the shipwreck site with the JASON robot. For two weeks, we would beam live broadcasts from the ocean floor to hundreds of thousands of school children in museums all over North America. The students would come with us as we explored a shipwreck and tested how robots could be used to help archaeologists. We also planned to investigate some fascinating underwater geology. We'd already found an active underwater volcano called Marsili Seamount, but we were still searching for our all-important lost ship.

Sitting in my office back at Woods Hole Oceanographic Institution on Cape Cod, Massachusetts, finding a wreck in the Mediterranean Sea had seemed like a piece of cake. On my huge wall map of the world's oceans, "the Med" looked like a little lake. Yet during ancient times it was crisscrossed by countless ships—Phoenician, Egyptian, Greek, Carthaginian, Roman. Shipwrecks were frequent—the ships were at the wind's mercy—and many sank in deep water, too deep for scuba divers but within reach of *Argo*. What's more, in the icy depths of the deep sea, where no sunlight can penetrate and sediment accumulates slowly, long-lost objects would lie untouched by time. So we hoped. But all we'd seen so far this year were six lonely amphoras, the big pottery jars the Romans used to transport cargo such as wine, oil, dried fish

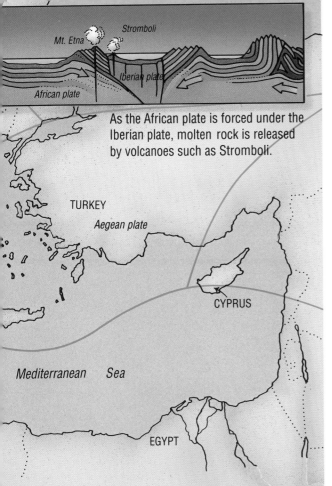

As the African plate is forced under the Iberian plate, molten rock is released by volcanoes such as Stromboli.

TURKEY

Aegean plate

CYPRUS

Mediterranean Sea

EGYPT

fitting the continents together like pieces of a puzzle. And the pieces are still drifting.

The Mediterranean basin is a very complex area that not only has plates colliding, but also has plates rubbing against each other just as they do along California's San Andreas Fault. This results in massive earthquakes that can cause equally massive destruction.

The pale blue square on the map shows the JASON Project study area.

and fish sauce. That sighting had been on June 3, the second day of our search, off the western tip of Sicily. But for the past several days, as we slowly worked our way eastward along the north coast of Sicily, following a route taken by countless ancient mariners, all we had seen were the marks of fishermen's trawler nets on the muddy bottom. It appeared that the Mediterranean had been scraped clean.

I was still watching Stromboli fade into the distance when the rest of the JASON team had returned to their bunks. Even though I knew I needed sleep too, I continued to stare out at the moonlit sea. The Mediterranean suddenly seemed huge, not a little lake but a great ocean.

We launch our search vehicle and camera sled, *Argo*, from the giant A-frame on the stern of the ship.

The next morning, we launched *Argo* near the mouth of the Strait of Messina. We knew that in ancient times, thousands of ships sailing to and from Rome and Naples had passed this way. Today we would follow this trade route north toward Naples. Surely, I told myself, we would find some evidence of ship-wrecks here.

As we tracked slowly northward from the Strait of Messina, the video screens in the control van contin-ued to show us nothing but bottom mud scarred with trawler marks. By the time the noon-to-four watch trooped into the van, I was really getting worried. Todd took his position at the *Argo* joystick control and Betsey, who was also on this watch, took her seat as data logger. Soon we were back within sight of Stromboli.

"Hey, what's that?" Todd was pointing at the video screen.

"Wow," chimed in Betsey, as we all looked at the suddenly different black-and-white TV picture.

Argo's cameras were showing us what seemed to be a giant crack in the ocean floor. It certainly wasn't a shipwreck, but it was a welcome change of scenery — and something of a mystery. The sea floor here was soft. What could be causing this crack?

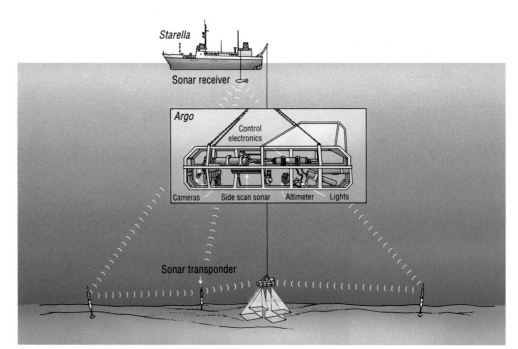

Starella

Sonar receiver

Argo

Control electronics

Cameras   Side scan sonar   Altimeter   Lights

Sonar transponder

(Right) We keep track of *Argo*'s position above the sea floor through the sonar signals it sends to the transponders. The transponders then send the signals to the ship's sonar receiver.

(Below) My son Todd and I get ready to launch *Argo* from the fantail of the *Starella*.

(Below right) *Argo* plunges into the water.

Then I remembered my trip to Iceland where I saw similar cracks around erupting volcanoes. "It's Stromboli. The volcano is breathing," I told Todd and Betsey. And strange as it may sound, that's a good description of what was happening. Deep inside every volcano is a big space called a magma chamber. Before an eruption, this space gradually fills with hot liquid rock, or magma, and the chamber begins to expand, stretching the area for miles around it. In this case the area included a muddy sea floor. It's as if you took a partially inflated balloon, covered it with a thin layer of mud and then put the balloon near a radiator or other heat source. The air in the balloon would expand

with the heat, and cracks would appear in the mud. If we'd been able to get a panoramic "aerial" view of Stromboli, we would have seen a network of these cracks all around the volcano.

Before long we'd left Stromboli's stretch marks behind and returned to our mind-numbing view of flat, featureless mud, interrupted only by the occasional crab or bottom fish.

"That's it, I've had it," I muttered to myself. We were now just off Naples, one of the busiest ports in Roman times. For more than a day we'd traced the trade route from Messina to Naples without seeing any sign of ancient shipping. We had looked everywhere

Our shipboard routine is interrupted when Betsey Robinson, Julie Loesch and I begin a water fight.

we expected to find a wreck and found nothing. Our only hope now was to go back to those six amphoras we'd seen at the beginning of our search. Maybe they would lead us to something bigger.

"Bring home *Argo*," I ordered, and Todd immediately pulled back on the joystick. As he did so, the big electric winch near the stern of the *Starella* began winding in *Argo*'s cable, slowly pulling our video vehicle back to the surface. The deck crew was already out on the stern making sure that the cable came back in smoothly. A snag could lead to later problems—

including a snapped cable and the loss of *Argo*. But so far, knock on wood, we'd escaped disaster.

I took one last look around the control van and then went out onto the afterdeck of the *Starella*. Soon we would be steaming full speed toward the Strait of Sicily, to an area marked on the chart as Skerki Bank, an underwater plateau that lay directly in the path of the main trade route between the ancient North African city of Carthage and Rome. This was our last chance to find a wreck from the ancient world.

Early the next morning, June 10, we were over Skerki Bank and approaching the area where we'd first seen those six amphoras. I gave the order for *Argo* to be lowered. I knew it was now or never.

Skerki Bank was the only area we'd seen in more than a week that showed few signs of the trawling that had scraped the bottom clean almost everywhere else. This underwater island of opportunity was roughly 200 square miles (520 square kilometres). That's a fair bit of territory to cover. So I'd decided to start looking right where we'd found those six amphoras. Maybe they were part of a debris field from a single wreck. If so, all we had to do was explore the area around them, and we'd find what we were looking for.

As we had discovered in looking for other deep-sea wrecks, a ship almost never sinks in one piece. Even if it does, it leaves a field of debris as it goes down — pieces of the hull, parts of the cargo and so on. The main hull of the ship and the heaviest items tend to fall straight down. The lighter pieces drift as they fall, carried by underwater currents. This creates a trail of debris that can be a mile or more long depending on the depth of the water and the strength of the currents. You can usually find the main chunks of a wreck by following the debris trail from lighter to heavier objects. This is what we hoped to do now.

Soon after *Argo* reached viewing altitude, we saw an amphora. Then we spotted another. Clearly we were in some kind of debris field, but which way was the ship? For the rest of the day and on into the night we "mowed the lawn" without running out of debris. Mowing the lawn is the term we use to describe a standard search pattern of parallel lines run one after the other. In this case each new line was a mile to the north of the previous one.

The next morning, when we finally found the northern limit, it was clear that this was no ordinary debris field. It was far too big for one shipwreck, and yet we'd seen no sign of a single wreck — just scatterings of cargo from many ancient ships.

For all I knew, a whole fleet of Roman ships had sunk here or, more likely, countless ships over hundreds of years. Perhaps a great sea battle had been fought here during the wars between Carthage and Rome. Whatever the case, I figured there had to be some sign of an actual ship sooner or later. So I decided to continue our search to the south of the area we'd just covered.

Around noon, Todd and Betsey's watch straggled into the control van and took up their positions. I gave them instructions to start our next line, then I stepped outside to get some air. It was a lovely summer day. The sea was calm, and off-duty crew members were sunbathing on the bow. It would have been a perfect day for a ship from Carthage to cross the Strait of Sicily, perhaps stop briefly at Trapani on the western tip of Sicily, then continue on toward Rome. But if a sudden storm had come up when the ship was far from land, it could have sunk without a trace.

(Below) We watch the video screens in the control van that show us what *Argo* sees hundreds of feet below.

(Right) Recovering *Argo*.

(Left) A celebration breaks out in the control van as objects from a Roman ship appear on our video screens.

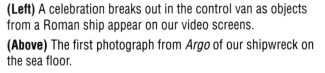

(Above) The first photograph from *Argo* of our shipwreck on the sea floor.

The sun was warm, and I let myself daydream about what it must have been like to be the master of one of those ancient wooden vessels over 100 feet (30 metres) from stem to stern. No navigation satellites to guide me, just the sun and the stars and the glow from Stromboli. No engine noises, no smelly diesel fuel, just the swooshing of wind in the sails, the creak of ropes and canvas, the shouts of sailors, perhaps the bleating and mooing of livestock being carried on deck. Times were certainly simpler then, the air cleaner, the waters unpolluted. But life was shorter, and the power of nature must have seemed immense. No wonder the Greeks and the Romans believed that the earth, the

sea and the sky were ruled by powerful gods who could help them or whose anger could hurl them to destruction.

Just after two p.m., I was chatting with members of the film crew from National Geographic Television when Betsey and Todd came rushing out of the van.

"We've got her! We've hit the mother lode! We've found a ship," they told me breathlessly. "We're sure we've got a ship."

I followed them back into the van at a run. Had we finally found what we were looking for?

But whatever Betsey and Todd had seen was long gone as the *Starella* obediently followed the course I'd laid out. At 2:05, when the objects first came into view, Betsey had scribbled into her data log, "at least nine amphoras in main heap." This sounded like a ship's cargo, but the freeze-frame video image was too fuzzy to be convincing. I ordered the navigator to take us back for another look. If it was a ship, I wanted a sharp photograph from *Argo*'s high-resolution still camera to prove it.

But finding our discovery a second time turned out to be quite a challenge. After all, we were looking for a heap of amphoras that would cover the floor of a small room. We'd been very lucky to stumble over it in the first place. Through the night and on into the next morning we searched and re-searched the area, continuing to miss the target — probably by only a few metres each time. Everyone on board was becoming very frustrated.

As the 8 a.m. to noon watch of June 12 passed its halfway point, I began to wonder if *Argo*'s cameras had showed us a mirage. Even though Todd wasn't on duty, he was hanging around the van, waiting for something to happen. But Betsey had finally given up and gone to bed so that she'd have had some sleep before her watch began at noon.

Just before 11 a.m., the watch navigator brought the *Starella* for the umpteenth time over the area where the wreck lay. Suddenly Todd let out a yell.

"That's it, we've found her!" he shouted.

All eyes were glued to the video screen as the cluster of debris came into view. I could see more than a dozen artifacts grouped together, mostly amphoras, but also other material, including what looked like a round grindstone. From the way they lay, it was clear they had fallen together. At long last we'd found our shipwreck.

As soon as the high-resolution still picture was developed, Todd rushed off to find Betsey, who certainly wouldn't mind being wakened. Inside the van the scene was one of quiet jubilation. I shook hands all round. Then I gave the orders to recover *Argo*. I wanted to leave the area largely unexplored so that next year we could give students a chance to participate in the thrill of being scientific explorers. And what better way to do that than to make discoveries before their very eyes! There was also lots of work to do before we would be ready to return with JASON for our live broadcasts from the Mediterranean sea floor.

Send it by amphora...

Amphoras are large two-handled clay jars used as shipping containers in ancient times. Their pointed "toes" or bottoms meant that a man could lift an amphora up on his shoulder and carry it. These toes also allowed amphoras to be stacked upright in tiers in the hold of a ship (**right**), while their round bodies meant they could be rolled around easily on the deck.

The Romans used these thick-walled jars to carry large quantities of liquid or food. Narrow-mouthed jars held wine, olive oil, fish sauce or honey. Wide-mouthed jars could carry dried fish or fruits, nuts or olives. Sometimes amphoras containing liquids were lined with a sticky resin to seal the baked clay and hold the liquid safely within. The mouth of the jar was tightly sealed with mortar and sometimes cork or terracotta stoppers were also used.

After the contents were finished, amphoras were often broken and left in great heaps. These broken pieces were often mixed in with building material, used as landfill, or even as small coffins for child burials. Amphoras are still used today in many parts of the Mediterranean.

CHAPTER TWO

The *Isis* Sets Sail · A.D. 355

"Watch where you're going!" yelled a rough-looking sailor, swearing under his breath in Greek.

Antonius, standing near the prow of the *Isis*, suddenly saw a battered ship heading straight at him. He watched in amazement as the *Isis* altered course at the last moment, narrowly missing the Greek. It all happened too quickly for him to feel afraid.

"It was our right of way, you idiot!" bellowed the captain of the *Isis*, who had grabbed the steering oars from his helmsman just in time. "May Neptune spit on you!" he cursed as the ships drew rapidly apart. A new breeze filled the sails and the ship picked up speed. "Stupid impatient Greek," he muttered. "He will not earn one *nummus* more by arriving at the dock five minutes early."

Leaving the crowded port of Ostia was never easy, what with hundreds of fishing boats and merchant ships jostling for space. But this morning navigation

A slave unloads a huge amphora from a merchant ship in this stone relief, carved in the third century A.D.

was even trickier because of the heavy mist that hung over the water.

Antonius watched the lighthouse and red brick warehouses of Ostia grow smaller and smaller then disappear in the haze. Although he had often ridden on the small boats that transported goods from Ostia up the Tiber River to Rome, this was his first real sea voyage. For years he had begged his father, the merchant Fabius, to let him come on a trading voyage, but his mother had always intervened, saying that he was far too young, that she could not bear to be parted from him for so long. But now he was fourteen, a man, and this time his mother could only shake her head sadly as his father agreed to let his son go with him. It was time for Antonius to learn the trade, Fabius told her.

The *Isis* was loaded with 5,000 amphoras filled with his father's wine and headed for the city of Carthage. Africa! It seemed so far away. There Fabius would sell his wine and load up with garum (a sauce made from the guts of fish), oil, grain, woven rugs and cloth goods, pottery, and maybe even some ivory and ebony. But they were also going to bring back a wild cat, if they could get one, for the games in the Colosseum, the most famous *amphitheatrum* in the Empire.

Antonius felt a hand on his shoulder. It was his father. "Your Aunt Claudia is driving me crazy with her complaining," Fabius told the boy. "I don't know why I agreed to let her come with us. Go back and see if you can distract her."

"Yes, sir," Antonius replied and headed toward the stern of the ship where he had last seen his aunt and Syra, her Christian slave, arranging their blankets and belongings, making their places on the deck as comfortable as possible.

Of all his aunts, Antonius liked Aunt Claudia, his father's younger sister, the best. She had never married but had had many adventures. When he was younger she had entertained him for hours with tales of the exotic places she had visited–the pyramids of Egypt and the Parthenon in Athens. Aunt Claudia had already seen the sights of Carthage, but wanted to buy some new carpets, and red pottery for her table. She also wanted to visit the Temple of Venus on Mount Eryx in Sicily on the return voyage.

Antonius threaded his way along the crowded deck. Every corner was crammed with people. There were many families with small noisy children that played gleefully together. A group of swarthy young men, going to the African city to seek work, joked amongst themselves. Antonius watched them with envy. Several government officials sat apart, talking quietly together, trying to ignore the piercing shrieks from the children.

Fabius points out a nearby ship to Antonius while two slaves work on the *Isis*. One stirs a pot of pine resin and another fastens rings to a sail.

Fish guts anyone?

The Romans enjoyed serving their food with garum, a smelly fish sauce made from the guts of fish, salted and left to ferment in the sun in huge jars. Garum, like our mustard or relish, was found on every Roman table and gave food its salty taste. Diluted with honey, wine or herbs, the Romans even drank it as a liquor or used it as a medicine. It was supposed to cure everything, from a crocodile bite to stomach cramps!

Because it took time and effort to make, garum was expensive. An amphora of the best garum cost ten times as much as an amphora of the finest wine.

The mosaic of sea creatures (**above**) is from Pompeii.

Many of the passengers were pilgrims who, like Aunt Claudia, wanted to visit the famous temple on Mount Eryx, where they would offer prayers and sacrifices to the goddess Venus. Slaves hastily set up makeshift shelters using walking sticks, blankets and whatever else they could find. Some of the passengers began to unpack baskets full of bread, cheese, fruit and wine, food which would have to last for several days. Everyone was happy to be under way at last.

"May the gods be with you, Aurelius." Antonius felt very grown-up as he greeted the tall, important-looking man who stood near the ship's mast giving orders to his slave.

"And with you," the man replied with a smile. Aurelius was a government official going to Carthage to check on the management of the olive oil business there. He had brought with him a new oil press. On the return trip he would bring back 4,000 amphoras full of highly-prized North African olive oil.

As Antonius approached the stern of the ship, he could hear his aunt's high-pitched voice.

The fretful Claudia tries to keep herself cool as Syra, her slave girl, searches for something to eat.

"Where is that foul smoke coming from?" Claudia said, pinching her nose in disgust. "Syra, fetch me my fan at once!" Syra rolled her brown eyes but began to search for the fan. A scrawny Syrian slave, who had just emerged from the nearby galley carrying a pot of steaming pine resin grinned at Antonius. He was used to the complaints of tourists, and the captain had ordered him to slather the smelly pine resin over all the cracks in the hull timbers.

"How beautiful you look, Aunt…," Antonius began.

"Don't be ridiculous, my boy," Claudia interrupted. "It is impossible to look one's best on a sea voyage. And this ship is the worst. Why, there's hardly enough room to move." With an indignant snort she tried to wave away a shabby-looking family of Sicilians who were about to settle themselves close by.

"I'm not feeling myself today, Antonius." Claudia sighed as Syra handed her a fan. "I think I'll rest for awhile. But come and talk to me later and I'll tell you about the first time I visited Carthage."

Antonius left his aunt to rest as Syra attempted to arrange pillows around her fanning, fretting mistress.

The wind from the north was growing stronger, filling out the mainsail and causing the ship to heel over and throw up spray as it plowed through the water. Antonius loved the gentle shudder each time the ship hit a wave and the way the spray sparkled in the sunlight. The morning mist had burned away and the sun was hot now, so the boy found a sheltered spot in the lee of the galley and sat dreamily watching the sky and the sea.

But soon his peaceful mood was interrupted by a strange sound nearby. It made him think of an old cow giving birth. Then he realized it was his Aunt Claudia moaning. She must be seasick. Antonius went to get his father.

Fabius shook his head in exasperation. "What's the matter with that sister of mine? I've never known her to be such a baby." When they found Claudia, her face was white with nausea and fear.

"We must go back, Fabius. I've never been seasick before. This is surely an ill omen."

"Don't talk such nonsense, Claudia. You'll just upset the boy. A little rest and you'll be fine."

Claudia let out another moan and turned her back to them. As Fabius and Antonius left her to suffer alone, Antonius noticed that his father's face was grim.

Then Antonius remembered a conversation he'd overheard the night before when he was supposed to be sleeping. The captain of the *Isis*, a wiry Sicilian who had sailed his father's ship many times, had come to their inn in Ostia.

"It's far too late in the year to be making this voyage. The stormy season could begin any time. You're risking your cargo—and the lives of all of us on board!"

But Fabius had not built up his fortune by being cautious. He was determined to make this one last trip to Carthage.

In the flickering lamplight the captain's harsh whisper had seemed part of a bad dream. Now his words seemed very real.

That day, as the *Isis* sailed south along the coast of Italy toward Puteoli, such fears seemed very far away. The weather remained sunny, Aunt Claudia's seasickness passed, and the captain showed no signs of concern. He even briefly let Antonius steer the ship under the watchful eye of the muscular helmsman. Perhaps the captain's words really had been a bad dream.

By late afternoon, Antonius was growing bored so he decided to explore below decks where the cargo was stored. The dark, damp hold of the *Isis* was a different world. In every direction were wine-filled amphoras packed layer upon layer and cushioned by twigs and branches to prevent the containers from breaking. Antonius ran his hand over their cool smooth surfaces, and then sat listening to the creaking of the hull and the slap of the waves against the timbers. Through the planks above him he could hear laughter and the buzz of different accents and dialects. Suddenly, feeling hungry, he scrambled up the ladder, back into the fresh air.

The sun was beginning to sink toward the horizon. It wouldn't be long until dinner, but he couldn't wait, so he made his way to the tiny galley at the stern of the ship. As he crouched to enter the low-roofed room that was lit by a single small oil lamp, the pungent smells of food and sweat greeted him. The galley slave, a large balding man, was singing loudly in Greek as he cleaned freshly-caught fish for the few privileged passengers on board–Fabius, Antonius, Claudia, Aurelius and the captain. He greeted Antonius with a nod.

"Dinner soon. You wait," he grunted as he chopped off the head of a large fish. Then softening slightly, he added, "But here, take bread, and little cup water from jug."

Dinner was worth the wait. The tender fish with its sauce of garlic, wine and olive oil seemed even more delicious than any meal he had eaten at home.

The following afternoon Antonius was back in his spot near the ship's prow. All he could see was the coast of Italy, a faint line on the horizon. If he leaned out over the side he could see the goddess Isis painted in gold on the ship's stempost.

The Greek galley slave prepares a fish that he will fry on a grill over the firebox.

Suddenly his eye caught a speck in the distance, something different from the waves and clouds and sky. He looked harder.

"A sail!" he cried out in excitement.

"Where? Where do you see a sail at this ungodly time of year?" growled the captain, who was standing on the bow deck.

"There!" Antonius pointed and the captain squinted, shielding his eyes with his hands.

"You may be right," he muttered. "Can you climb, boy?"

"Yes, sir," Antonius answered.

"Then get up that ladder and have a better look."

Antonius wasted no time–even though his father had forbidden him from climbing up the mast. With trembling legs he clambered up the swaying ladder.

This Roman stone relief shows three ships arriving in Ostia. In the confusion of nearing port one sailor has fallen overboard.

Finally, gasping for breath, he stood on the pitching yard while he hugged the top of the mast. He didn't dare look down as he strained to see whether there really was a ship in the distance or if it was just the play of the light on the sea.

"Do you see a sail?" came the captain's voice.

There it was!

"Yes," he shouted back excitedly, almost forgetting to hold onto the mast. "It looks green!" Antonius felt a pounding in his ears. He knew that a green sail could only mean a pirate ship. Pirates' sails were always green or blue to camouflage themselves against the water. Sailors feared pirate attacks even more than dangerous cooking fires that sometimes spread from a ship's galley. Once pirates caught up with a ship, they boarded and tied everyone up. If Roman citizens dared to protest that they were not slaves, the pirates would apologize, pretending that all was well, and then force them to walk the ship's ladder over the side. Those who kept their mouths shut were sold as slaves in a foreign port.

"Get out of our way, boy!" Two sailors had joined Antonius at the mast tip, sent aloft to untie the topsail. Antonius somehow found the strength to climb back down to the deck. There other sailors were hoisting the foresail. The *Isis* would need every stitch of canvas if she were to outrace the pirate ship.

Soon the *Isis* was heeling over sharply as the extra sails caught the wind. Waves washed over the leeward rail as the ship plunged forward, moving as fast as the wind could take it. Some of the passengers were screaming in fear. A baby started wailing. Everyone clung to anything solid as their bundles of clothing and blankets slid across the sloping deck.

Antonius gripped the rail with both hands as the salt spray lashed his face. But he couldn't take his eyes off the pirate ship. Spellbound, he stared at the green sail as it became smaller and smaller. Before long it was out of sight, and there was nothing to be seen but blue-green water and the sun in the sky. The crew eased off on the sails, the ship righted itself, and the passengers began to gather their scattered possessions.

But the captain and his second in command, the sailing master, still looked concerned as they pored over a navigation handbook. The *Isis* had lost sight of land in her desperation to leave the pirate ship far behind. But to head back toward land meant heading back in the direction they'd last seen the pirates. So they sailed south for several hours, guided only by the glowing sun. As darkness fell, Antonius could see that the captain and sailing master had become tense and silent. The hairs prickled on the back of his neck as he realized that they were no longer sure where they were.

Antonius was awakened by the sound of the sailors calling to one another. He sat up and listened for the sound of his father's breathing next to him. Nothing.

Rubbing his eyes, he stumbled to the foredeck. The scene that met him was like a carnival. Everyone on board was awake and most had crowded toward the bow of the *Isis*. People were talking and laughing and pointing. Puzzled and excited, Antonius began to search for his father and Aunt Claudia.

"The gods are angry," an old man muttered as he passed.

"Nonsense," his wife replied. "That's Stromboli."

At last Antonius saw what everyone was looking at. Off in the distance was a red glow in the sky. Occasionally it grew brighter or almost faded out. So this was the famous volcano of Stromboli.

"Antonius, what are you doing up at this time of night?" Aunt Claudia's voice was sharp, but her eyes sparkled. In fact, she seemed to be in wonderful spirits, leaning out over the rail to get a good view. Even Fabius and Aurelius seemed to be enjoying themselves.

"Did I ever tell you about the first time I saw Stromboli?" Claudia continued. "I was a girl of sixteen, sailing with your grandfather on my first sea voyage. We were going to Alexandria with a hold full of good red wine. In Egypt grandfather planned to buy grain to bring back to Rome."

Antonius grinned. It was hard to imagine middle-aged Aunt Claudia as a girl of sixteen.

"There was a young centurion on board the ship, going to rejoin his legion in Judea. He was very handsome…"

At that moment the volcano spewed hot lava and ash. Some people in the crowd shrieked. Antonius thought he had never seen anything so beautiful, or so frightening.

"…and *very* hotblooded," Claudia continued, as she toyed dreamily with one of her many silver bracelets. "Father certainly had his hands full keeping an eye on me the night we passed Stromboli."

Several hours later, with Stromboli's red glow now growing distant off the stern, the passengers straggled back to their places on the deck.

"Come to bed soon," Fabius said to his son, as he and Claudia turned to go. "We have a long day ahead of us tomorrow."

As dawn approaches, the weary helmsman carefully steers the *Isis* back on course.

Soon the ship was quiet. But Antonius was determined to stay awake. He picked his way over sleeping bodies and piles of belongings to the stern, and perched near the helmsman so that he could watch Stromboli as it became a tiny red speck in the distance. Soon the helmsman and the sailing master were the only ones still awake as the gentle night breeze carried the *Isis* westward.

"Once we saw Stromboli, I knew we had to alter course," explained the sailing master. "If we'd continued south we might have run smack into one of the islands off the north coast of Sicily. Tomorrow we'll pick up fresh water at Motya. The day after that, we'll be in Carthage."

The next thing Antonius knew it was morning. Sunlight was streaming across the deck, and he could hear the high-pitched call of gulls, a sure sign they were close to land.

CHAPTER THREE

Near Disaster · 1989

By early April 1989, the second phase of the JASON Project was ready to begin. The JASON robot was almost finished. Twelve museums in the United States and Canada and 250,000 students had arranged to watch our live broadcasts from the Mediterranean. During the week of May 1, we would broadcast from Marsili Seamount while we observed this active underwater volcano. During the following week, our broadcast site would be just north of Skerki Bank as we explored the Roman shipwreck we'd discovered during the 1988 expedition.

With JASON's robot arm, we would be able to pick up rock and animal samples from the volcano. Later, we planned to recover amphoras and other archaeological material from the ancient ship under the direction of Dr. Anna McCann, the professional archaeologist who had joined our team.

Most of the JASON team had boarded our ship, the *Star Hercules*, in England. The time sailing to the Mediterranean would be spent putting finishing touches on JASON and his specially designed garage and camera sled, called *Hugo* — or *Huge Argo*. As usual, we were going to sea with new technology that would be tested in action.

In mid-April I joined the ship in the port of Gibraltar at the entrance to the Mediterranean Sea. The scene that greeted me when I stepped on board the *Star Hercules* was not a pretty one. The JASON team was still green after a scary passage across the Bay of Biscay from England to Gibraltar. They'd been buffeted by a terrible storm with thirty-foot waves and fifty to sixty knot gusts of wind. And to make matters worse, they'd been hit by a rogue wave, a mountain of water that comes out of nowhere with no warning. Equipment lashed near the stern had broken loose, crashing into vans and pummelling *Hugo*, which now looked like it had been attacked by an angry sea monster. The electronics van was the worst hit — it had flooded with seawater, ruining a lot of the computers, and its floor had buckled. In addition, the storm had prevented the

JASON, our state-of-the-art underwater robot, can dive as deep as 20,000 feet (6,100 metres), while the safety limit for deep diving with scuba is only 130 feet (40 metres).

1 Tubular frame
2 Electronics and wiring
3 Side scan sonar
4 Thruster (1 of 7)
5 Electronic compass
6 Emergency locator beacon
7 Forward scanning sonar
8 Still camera and flash
9 Video camera (1 of 3)

(Top) Our workshop vans on the deck of the *Star Hercules*.
(Above) JASON sits snugly inside *Hugo*.
(Right) Sunbathing on the roof of the computer van.

technicians from doing the final work needed to make JASON ready for launching. Our team was tired and behind schedule. The situation looked hopeless.

JASON *had* to be ready. He was the "swimming eyeball" that would be linked to *Hugo* by a 500-foot (150-metre) tether. His cameras would send back clear and close-up video pictures of the sea floor, and his sophisticated propulsion system would allow us to manipulate him right up to our target. In short, we were depending on JASON to bring underwater exploration alive for our school audiences.

On April 20, we left the Rock of Gibraltar, bound for Skerki Bank. Once we reached it, we'd have less than a week to get ready for our first live TV show. If the good weather held, we should have no problems.

I prayed that Isis, the Egyptian goddess who protected sailors, would look after us. Isis was also the goddess of the afterlife, and she was worshipped by the Romans. In fact, our archaeologist, Dr. Anna

McCann, suggested that Isis was a perfect name for the shipwreck we'd found.

But the weather grew steadily worse as we approached Skerki Bank increasing my worries about *Hugo*. The afternoon before we were to arrive at the *Isis* site, I made my way aft to the fantail to see how the team was doing with *Hugo* and JASON. Andy Bowen, the chief engineer, was bent over *Hugo*'s massive aluminum frame. He was so wrapped up in his work that he didn't seem to notice the heaving of the ship or the occasional cold shower of salt spray.

"I still don't like it," I commented to Andy. "This thing is a monster." *Hugo* measured four times the size of the old *Argo*. Its bulk was necessary, at least in part, so it could serve as a garage for JASON. But *Hugo* was even bigger than we had planned. I thought the vehicle was just too big. If it was launched in rough seas, as the ship rose on a swell, *Hugo* would still be falling from the last trough. This could cause what we call snap loading, when the cable strains as the ship is going one way and *Hugo* the other. I was worried that *Hugo* would snap its brand-new fiber-optic cable before it had even had a chance to fly.

Skip Gleason lends a hand as the monstrous *Hugo*, with JASON inside, is lowered from the A-frame.

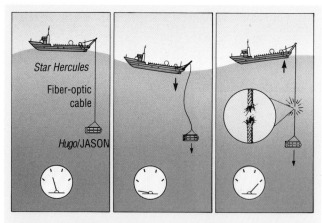

Star Hercules

Fiber-optic cable

Hugo/JASON

As we lower *Hugo* from the ship, there is a 10,000 lb (4,500 kg) stress on *Hugo*'s cable. When the ship descends into a trough between waves, the cable goes slack since there is no stress on it (as the gauge **above** shows). But when the ship is carried up again by the next wave, *Hugo* is still falling, and a 22,000 lb (10,000 kg) stress on the cable causes it to snap, sending *Hugo* crashing to the bottom.

"Don't worry, Bob," Andy reassured me. "Our new baby will do fine."

My gut told me otherwise, but I figured I was stuck with *Hugo*. It would just have to work.

* * *

"Dr. Ballard, we have you on screen. All museums have signed on. Countdown to air: 5, 4, 3, 2, 1." The voice was from the Turner Broadcasting control room in Atlanta, Georgia, telling me that half a world away, staff people in twelve museums would be watching. It was April 26, and this was our first dry run for the live TV broadcasts that would begin for the students on May 1.

"Good morning from the Mediterranean," I began cheerfully. "You've tuned in just in time to see a live launch of *Hugo* and JASON."

As I talked, out of the corner of my eye I watched the video screen that monitored *Hugo*'s cable. This was the first time JASON would fly from *Hugo*, and our new fiber-optic cable would be subjected to more snap-loading pressure than ever before. I was very nervous. Although the worst of the storm was over, the sea swells were still high. What a time to be performing for the TV cameras!

"We've got the vehicle in the water now. As you can see from the video screen behind me, the cable is

going out smoothly. It will take about thirty minutes for *Hugo* to make the descent to the bottom, a distance of roughly half a mile."

Suddenly, as the ship's stern descended into a trough between swells, I saw the cable go slack. I braced myself for the strain I knew was about to come. Then as the ship rose with the next swell the video screens in the control van went blank! In that instant I knew that the cable had snapped. Millions of dollars of equipment were crashing toward the sea floor.

"Oh, my god!" I shouted, completely forgetting I was on television. I tore off my microphone headset and dashed from the van, leaving Turner Broadcasting to explain what had happened to astonished museum workers across North America.

My first thought was for the safety of the deck crew. When a cable breaks under intense strain, it snaps back like a huge whip with enough force to kill. Fortunately, the crew had seen the cable go slack and had cleared out of the way in time. Now they were milling around the fantail in a state of shock. So were the *Hugo* and JASON engineers.

I had to do something, so I just began giving orders. It made me feel better and it got people moving. But all the time I was thinking that somehow we had to get JASON back in time for the television shows. But how?

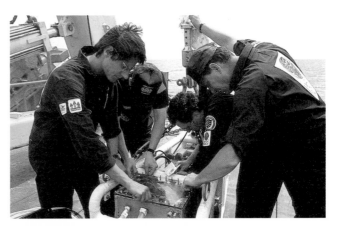

(Left) The broken cable on the empty deck.

(Above) JASON team members hurriedly prepare our back-up vehicle *Medea* for the rescue.

I'd already decided one thing: I was never putting *Hugo* back in the water. It was just too big. That meant we needed a lighter vehicle that could rescue JASON and then replace *Hugo* during the TV programs. I turned toward Bill Hersey, my top electrical engineer, who was standing nearby.

"Bill," I shouted. "Get *Medea* over here." *Medea* was a back-up vehicle we'd brought along just in case. We'd built it to test the fiber-optic cable, but never in our wildest dreams had we intended it to support JASON. *Medea* was named after the princess the original Jason had fallen in love with during his quest for the golden fleece. *Medea*'s sorcery had helped the Greek hero survive his trials and capture the fleece. Well, our modern-day JASON needed Medea's magic now. But first Bill Hersey would have to turn himself into a sorcerer.

Bill and I stood over *Medea* while I told him what I wanted him to do. I wanted cameras, lights,

everything—a mini-*Hugo* without that awkward garage. So right there on the spot Bill took out a pad of paper and began to design the new improved *Medea*—the wiring circuit, the camera circuit, the JASON hook-up. In about ten minutes he designed a whole new vehicle.

"How long have I got, Bob?" he asked.

"Twenty-four hours," I replied, knowing I was asking the impossible.

No one got much sleep that night. When I got up the next morning I could immediately tell from the motion of the *Star Hercules* that another storm was brewing. I splashed some cold water on my face and headed back to the scene of the battle.

In the electronics van, Bill Hersey and his team of technicians had worked through the night, and their JASON Project jumpsuits were black with grease. Cables and pieces of electronic equipment overflowed in the cramped space. Outside, *Medea* was a mangled mess. It didn't look like there was any hope, but Bill was confident.

"Oh, yeah, no problem," he assured me. "She'll be ready on time—but there's no way we can launch her in this storm."

The ship's deck was sopping with seawater, and I slipped and nearly went flying as I made my way back to the control van. Inside, however, the scene was one of calm efficiency. Dana Yoerger, robot computer whiz and chief navigator, greeted me with a gleam in his eye.

"Well, you'll be glad to hear that we know where *Hugo* and JASON are," he announced. "Both transponders are working and we can even tell you exactly which way *Hugo* is oriented."

This was good news. The transponders are underwater sonar beacons. If they'd been damaged, finding JASON would have been even tougher. Now the recovery was possible—if the weather would calm down.

"By the way," Dana added, "I can tell you exactly how fast *Hugo* fell. Four miles an hour."

"Saved by the drag," I grinned. For the first time I was grateful that *Hugo* was so big and presented so much water resistance. A smaller, heavier vehicle would have fallen faster and might well be buried in the mud. Since *Hugo* had descended so slowly, it was likely it had sunk only a little into the soft bottom.

The next day and a half were agony as we waited for the storm to die down. The clock kept ticking toward our broadcast deadline. The deadline was made even tighter by the fact that our first week of shows was scheduled to start 70 miles (110 kilometres) away at the Marsili Seamount. While the weather got worse,

---

In the hero bucket I manage to attach a hook and line to *Hugo*.

we hid in the lee of an island off Trapani, at the western tip of Sicily. As Bill Hersey had promised, *Medea* was soon ready to go, but the Mediterranean wouldn't cooperate.

On the morning of April 29, with only two days to our first broadcast, we could wait no longer. The weather was still awful as we pounded back out to Skerki Bank. Then, just as we approached the site, the storm broke. The winds dropped, the sun came out and the seas began to go down. There was still a big swell, but there was no time to lose. If we wanted to get JASON back, we'd have to risk losing *Medea*. It was all or nothing.

For the launch and rescue we assembled our crack team in the control van. Dana was on navigation and Martin Bowen (no relation to Andy), one of our best flyers, was in the driver's seat. As *Medea* approached the bottom, Martin's grip on the joystick tightened and all eyes were glued to the video monitor linked to *Medea*'s down-looking camera. At 200 feet (60 metres), a small light rectangle appeared smack in the middle of the screen. Sure enough it was *Hugo*, with JASON still snug inside. *Hugo* was upright and only slightly embedded in the mud. Dana had done his job to perfection. We made a couple of reconnaissance passes to check out all the angles.

"Okay, let's go and get it," I told Martin.

He promptly pushed forward on the joystick and *Medea*, her grappling hook dangling below her, dropped downward.

The swell on the surface was causing *Medea* to heave up and down with the motion of the *Star Hercules*. This would make it very difficult to get the hook into the bridle on top of *Hugo*. But if anyone could do it, Martin could.

The next thing we knew, the grappling hook had caught onto the frame on the port side of the vehicle and up *Hugo* went, twisting and turning like a wild animal. When Martin tried to lower it, the bottom mud was kicked up so that we couldn't see a thing. Here we were with a bucking bronco on the end of our rope and a blind cowboy trying to rein it in. There was nothing we could do but pull *Hugo* up, with our hook on the frame, and hope.

(Left) *Hugo* comes crashing up to the surface, but seconds later JASON escapes.

(Above) The Zodiac crew chases after JASON.

The ascent was hair-raising. Twice I watched in horror as *Medea*'s video camera showed the grappling hook come free on a downswell and then miraculously hook back onto *Hugo*'s frame as the ship rode up the next wave. Shivers went up my spine as each snap load exceeded the strain the cable was supposed to take. The same cable that had broken carrying only *Hugo* and JASON now had three vehicles in tow. Slowly but surely, however, *Medea* and her precious cargo moved up toward the surface. It took about half an hour. It seemed like an eternity.

I was out on the fantail with the deck team when *Medea* broke the surface and rose out of the water to the top of the A-frame, swinging dangerously as the ship rose and fell. Then *Hugo* appeared, still thrashing about in the water like a wild, untamed beast. I dashed to the "hero bucket," a small cage suspended from the stern that would allow me to get close to *Hugo* without being washed into the sea.

"Throw me a line," I shouted, as the waves crashed over me. Somehow I managed to get a hook into *Hugo*'s bridle, then get a line attached. Soon we had the vehicle secure against the side of the hull.

But as soon as *Hugo* cleared the water, JASON, which had been crashing around inside *Hugo* like a two-ton bowling ball, broke out of his cage and disappeared under the ship.

"Prepare to launch the Zodiac," I yelled at the closest member of the ship's crew and charged for the inflatable rubber boat lashed amidships. I still don't know how we launched the Zodiac into the wind, with the seas banging us back against the hull. Then the motor wouldn't go into gear so we had to row frantically out to JASON, which had now surfaced. Finally I got a hook and line on JASON and we brought him safely home.

But there was no time to relax. In less than twenty-four hours we were supposed to be on air with our first broadcast, and we had some ocean to cover and a lot of work to do before we could start sending live television pictures to the other side of the Atlantic Ocean.

CHAPTER FOUR

Live From the Marsili Seamount

"Hello, I'm Bob Ballard. We're in a special control room aboard the research vessel *Star Hercules*. For the next forty minutes we want you to share in an exciting undersea adventure using advanced robot systems. But before we begin our voyage of discovery, let me show you exactly where we are…"

It was the fifth day of our live broadcasts from the Marsili Seamount, six shows a day, and this was our twenty-seventh show. Our first broadcast had been a little shaky, but by now my colleagues and I were definitely getting the hang of things as thousands of students back home explored with us the underwater biology and geology of the area.

The Marsili Seamount is an active underwater volcano. If you could see it from ground level at a distance it would look very much like a volcano on land, with steeply sloping sides and a sharp peak. We saw evidence of underwater eruptions—formations known as pillow lavas, caused when the molten rock, or lava, cooled quickly as it entered the cold seawater.

But the most exciting evidence that the volcano was still very much alive was our discovery of hydrothermal vents, or hot springs beneath the sea floor—the first ever found in the Mediterranean Sea.

Martin Bowen, flying JASON, and *Star Hercules* navigator Dana Yoerger were trying to manipulate the two vehicles so that JASON's tether was in no danger of snagging on one of the upjutting chimneys that dotted this treacherous landscape. We were exploring part of the summit of Marsili, at a depth of about 1,000 feet (300 metres), that was crowded with jagged chimneys formed by the hot springs.

"We're in very rugged terrain," Martin commented tensely, as JASON's video camera seemed almost to touch a green and gold outcrop.

The JASON Project team prepares for our first live broadcast.

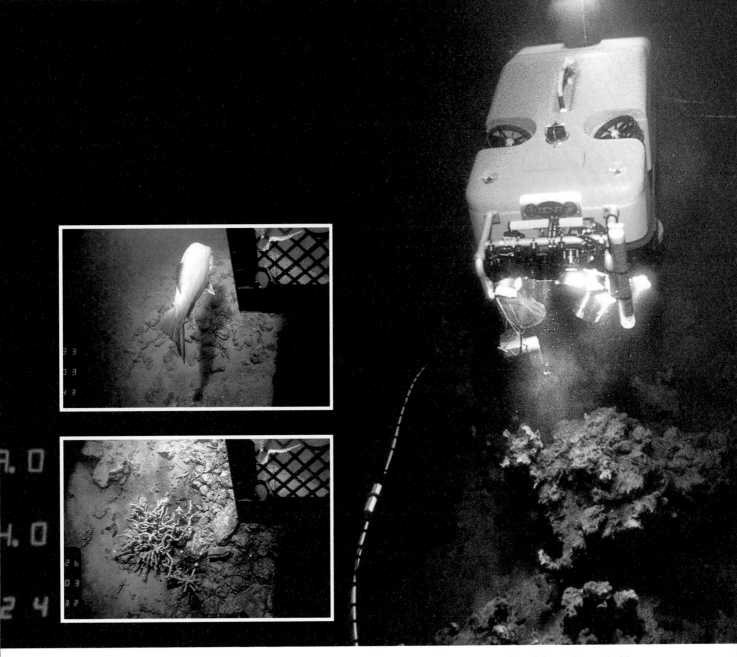

(Above) As JASON explores mineral deposits created by sea floor hot springs on top of the Marsili Seamount, a large fish (top inset) is drawn to JASON's lights and yellow sea anemones (bottom inset) rest on branching coral.

"Look at this!" exclaimed Dana. "We've got shimmering water!" Clearly visible on the screen was a plume of hot water entering the cold bottom water from the chimney vent.

All this was happening live. What we were seeing in the control van was also being witnessed by our television audience in North America. While Martin, Bob Elder, flying *Medea*, and Dana tried to get JASON close enough to the hot water to measure its temperature, I explained to our audience how the chimneys were formed.

"Seawater seeped down cracks in the volcano, and as it neared the magma chamber, it became super-hot and absorbed great quantities of minerals. As the hot mineral-rich water escaped through a vent, it came in contact with the cold bottom water, and the cooled mineral deposits created these tall chimney-shaped formations. The water coming out of the chimneys now is not nearly as hot as it was when they were formed."

At this point in the program I turned away from the live action on the sea floor to take some questions from the television audience. Many students were curious about telepresence—what it is and how it works. This is one of the questions I love to answer, because telepresence is one of my dreams come true.

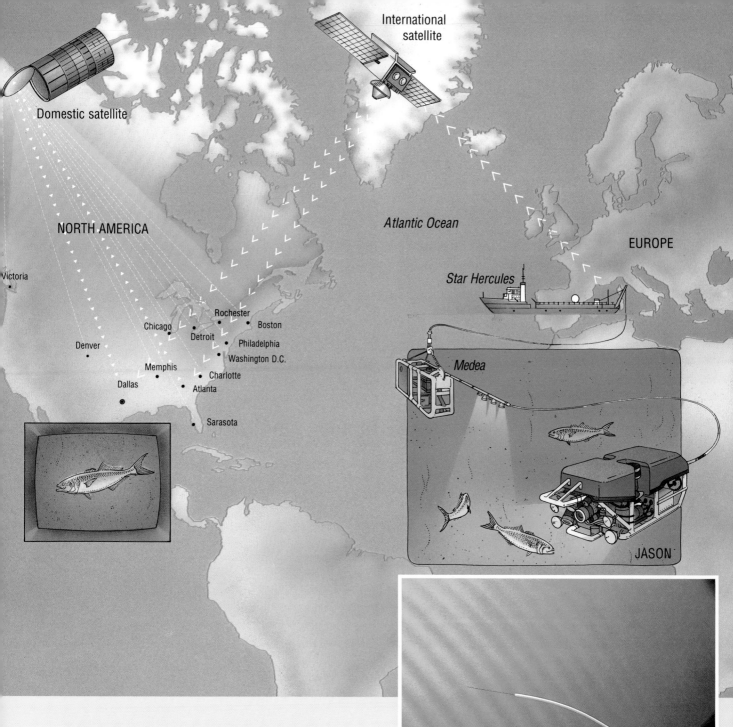

Domestic satellite

International satellite

NORTH AMERICA

Atlantic Ocean

EUROPE

Victoria

Rochester

Chicago • Boston

Detroit

Denver • Philadelphia

Washington D.C.

Memphis

Charlotte

Dallas • Atlanta

Sarasota

Star Hercules

Medea

JASON

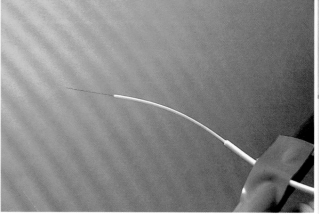

A Live Broadcast from the Sea Floor

What JASON sees with his video eyes is sent along his tether to *Medea*. *Medea* then relays the signal up her towing cable to the mother ship. Both the tether and the towing cable are fiber-optic cables. They contain thin strands of glass no wider than a human hair **(inset)** that transmit minute beams of light — microscopic lasers that carry the information our computers translate into pictures.

A fraction of a second after the image leaves JASON it appears on the screen in the control van. The next stop for the signals is the production van next door that is outfitted as a television control room. Then the images travel to an antenna on the stern of the ship that transmits the signals to a satellite orbiting 22,000 miles (35,000 kilometres) above the earth.

A transponder on that satellite retransmits the signals to earth where they are received by Turner Broadcasting System Inc. in Atlanta, Georgia, and by the EDS Information Management Center near Dallas, Texas. At Turner Broadcasting, another production team adds titles and pre-recorded material. An uplink truck then sends the program to a domestic satellite, which transmits the signals to museums in the JASON network. This journey of roughly 88,000 miles (140,000 kilometres) takes slightly less than half a second.

(Left) Broadcasting from the control van.

(Top) With our live satellite hook-up, students could ask me questions about the JASON Project as it was happening.

(Above) A replica of the control van on board our ship was created in each museum.

"Telepresence, or 'television presence', is a technology that enables me on board my research ship or you sitting in a museum thousands of miles away to experience the feeling of being in a submarine at the bottom of the sea. JASON and *Medea* send pictures from the sea floor through fiber-optic cables to the ship, and these images are then transmitted by satellite to you. Very soon you will be able to sit at home and explore the deep oceans with us.

Perhaps someday, using similar technology, you'll be able to visit Mars without leaving your house. Right now, however, this technology means that scientists back at Woods Hole or other institutions can participate in our expeditions without leaving their labs. They can analyze the data we collect and send their analyses back to us. So we can have a vast team of scientists — archaeologists, biologists, geologists — participating in our voyage without having to feed them or find them a bunk on the ship. This technology will make oceanography far more efficient and much less expensive."

All too soon, after a few more questions, it was time to bring the show to a close. In twenty minutes the next show would begin. By that time another 5,000 students would be ready to join us in our live exploration of the geology and biology of the Marsili Seamount at the bottom of the Tyrrhenian Sea.

CHAPTER FIVE

Home from Carthage · A.D. 355

"Gather up the mainsail. Prepare for docking!" The *Isis* was a beehive of activity as sailors clambered up the mast or coiled the mooring ropes. Skilfully the helmsman guided the ship through the many small skiffs and fishing boats that dotted the waters of the Carthage port. Then, ever so slowly, he brought her alongside the stone pier as lines were thrown ashore and made fast.

Antonius watched all this activity from his usual spot near the prow. He tried to take in everything at once. The docks were noisy and bustling with hundreds of slaves loading and unloading cargo. Several muscular men struggled with a huge slab of shining marble. Shipping clerks counted amphoras from another incoming ship and made entries in their ledgers. Dark-skinned fishermen sat on the docks mending their nets, oblivious to all the activity around them. A company of Roman soldiers tramped by.

Further off, the red tile roofs of the African city shimmered in the hot afternoon sun. Antonius could see the noble white columns of the Temple of Serapis up on a hill. And he could just glimpse the *amphitheatrum*—not as big as the Colosseum, but still impressive, and the circus where horse races took place. The great university was in the distance. Syra squeezed in beside Antonius to see the basilica of Saint Cyprian where she hoped to worship. Claudia still believed in the ancient gods, but she had nevertheless promised to help Syra find her way to the famous Christian church.

It would take the rest of the day for the slaves to unload his father's amphoras. That meant there was time to explore the city. Antonius rushed up to Fabius and Claudia, who were standing near the gangway.

"I think Antonius should come with me," Claudia was saying. "He will learn far more from a tour of

Relaxing Roman Style

The public baths were an important part of Roman life. People went to the baths not only to bathe, but to meet and talk with friends, to read, and to listen to musical performances or learned discussions. There were also swimming pools, grounds for exercising and wrestling, and courts for ball games. The baths were often beautifully decorated with mosaics and sculpture. The mosaic floor (right) can be seen today at the Baths of the Seven Sages in Ostia.

The baths were open to rich and poor alike, with separate areas or hours for

women. Bathers brought their own linen towels, oil and scrapers called strigils. And they usually took their slaves with them to watch their clothes, help them bathe, scrape them and give them a massage.

To heat the baths, a slave stoked a furnace with charcoal. The furnace heated tanks of water, and this water was piped into each room. The furnace also spread hot air through the hypocaust, a system of heating ducts under the hollow floors. The floors were supported by small columns of bricks as shown in the bottom corner of the picture (opposite page).

Fabius strikes a deal with the Carthaginian wine merchant, Gildo, in the lavishly decorated *caldarium* or hot bath.

the city than soaking in your silly baths or playing ninepins!"

"But much business is conducted at the baths," Fabius responded. "And there we are likely to meet people of importance in Carthage. Now that he is a man, Antonius must take on the responsibilities of manhood. He should come with me."

"If he is such a man, then let *him* decide," Aunt Claudia replied tartly. "What do *you* want to do, Antonius?"

Antonius looked at his aunt, then at his father's frowning face. He was dying to see the sights, but he also wanted to impress Fabius.

"I will go with my father," he finally replied. "But perhaps later, Aunt Claudia, we can go to the temple together — and the *amphitheatrum*."

"Very well," said Claudia, briskly turning her back to him as she looked around for Syra. "I want to do some shopping and Carthage has one of the finest markets in Africa. Syra! Where has that girl gone to? Bring me my purse and my fan."

Antonius felt very grown up as he strode with his father along the docks to the Antonine Baths that sat right on the waterfront. They were as big as the baths in Rome, and his father had told him they contained beautiful mosaics.

"Do you want to lift weights?" Antonius asked as they walked through the arched entrance and headed for the dressing room. Fabius almost always lifted weights at the baths in Rome.

"No, I'm too tired for exercise. Besides, I know where we will find the merchant who has promised to buy my wine. Since it is afternoon, Gildo is sure to be soaking in the *caldarium*."

Fabius had warned Antonius that Gildo was fat, but nothing prepared the boy for the glistening mountain of flesh that sat blissfully in the steaming hot water. The Carthaginian merchant's eyes were closed, his arms were folded, and he had a dreamy smile on his face.

"Only a rich man could afford to eat so much and work so little," Fabius whispered. Then in a louder voice, he continued, "Greetings, Gildo. May the gods smile on your enterprises and increase your wealth a thousandfold."

Gildo's eyes slowly opened, and his dreamy smile turned into a broad grin. "Fabius, you old fool," he laughed. "I never thought you would really risk a trip so late in the year. This will make your fortune."

The two friends quickly fell into an easy conversation, asking about each other's families, recounting their business ups and downs and chuckling together over past encounters. When it came to the bargaining, however, both were suddenly very serious.

"I couldn't possibly accept less than 8,000 *nummi* for each amphora," Fabius protested. "This is the finest wine from Latium, and I assure you it's the last shipment you will see in Carthage this year."

"Even so," Gildo replied sternly, "my cellars are already full. I will give you 6,000 *nummi* and not one *nummus* more."

The conversation continued in this vein until they had settled on a price of 7,000 *nummi*. Then they shook hands and agreed to meet later at Gildo's shop in the market. They were soon laughing and reminiscing again, as if the negotiation had never happened.

When Fabius and Antonius could take the heat no longer, they left Gildo still soaking and made their way to the *frigidarium*, where they refreshed themselves in the cold water. Then they covered themselves with oil and scraped themselves clean with a strigil. Invigorated and in high spirits, they set off to find Claudia.

After the peacefulness of the baths, the market was a dizzying whirl of sights, smells and activity. People were everywhere, many dressed in strange garb and speaking not in Latin or Greek, but in the many dialects of the native Berbers, and in Punic — the language of the ancient Phoenicians. A Berber woman with a bright blue shawl over her head cooked spicy-smelling meat stew over a griddle. A knot of people had formed around a juggler who kept three gold balls in the air at

once. A farmer sold eggs and chickens from the back of his cart. Another had a stall full of cabbages, turnips and melons. Slaves hurried everywhere — some buying food for dinner while others collected water from the public fountain, gracefully carrying the jugs on their heads. In a round building in the middle of the market, rows and rows of freshly-caught fish stared back at shoppers. Street musicians wove in and out of the market stalls playing pipes and cymbals, collecting what small coins they could.

Antonius and Fabius wandered from stall to stall admiring and sampling a variety of goods. "I know where we will find your aunt," Fabius said at last, as he took Antonius by the arm. "At the cloth merchant's. Claudia promised to buy me some of the fine cloth brought over the trade routes from Leptis Magna. It will fetch a high price in Rome."

Just as Fabius spoke, someone brushed against his side and dashed off into the crowd. Automatically he grabbed for the purse that always hung from his belt. It was gone.

"Stop, thief! Stop!" he shouted. "That man has stolen my purse!"

Without thinking, Antonius dashed off in pursuit. The thief was wearing a white turban, and Antonius could see it bobbing ahead of him as he pushed his way through the throng. Soon the crowds thinned and he had to run at full tilt to keep up. The turban darted down a side street. There were very few people now and the streets became narrower as the thief led the boy on a twisting, turning chase. Then the turban disappeared into a narrow alley. When Antonius got there, he found it empty. He walked on, peering at each shuttered window, until he came to a dead end. The white turban had disappeared.

Cursing, Antonius returned to the street and began retracing his steps toward the market. Now that he was no longer running, he could see that he was surrounded by huge, forbidding warehouses.

Antonius realized that he was lost. Each turn he took led him onto an unfamiliar street. And the only people he encountered either didn't understand Latin or were too afraid to speak to him. He began to worry. His father had warned him that many people

In the busy Carthage marketplace, Fabius and Antonius stop to sample some of the garum they may take back to Rome.

in Carthage were discontented with the rule of Rome. How would these people treat a lost Roman boy? He thought of his father and aunt. They would be frantic. Only a few hours ago he had felt like such a man, helping his father conduct business. Now he felt very young and afraid.

Suddenly, off in the distance he heard the roar of a crowd and the sound of trumpets. What could be happening? Then it hit him. The games! He had seen the bills posted at the baths:

In celebration of the holiday,
gladiators and venatores
from the school at Alexandria will fight.
Awnings will be used and there
will be sprinkling of perfume.

Antonius followed the shouts of the crowd. If he could find the *amphitheatrum*, he was sure he would be able to make his way back to the docks. Besides, there would be Roman soldiers there and other people who could speak his language. As the crowd noises grew louder, he began to run.

Antonius was running so fast that he charged right into a Roman legionnaire, who caught his shoulder in a vice-like grip.

"Where are you going in such a hurry, boy?" the soldier asked him sternly. "Perhaps you are the one who stole the purse from a Roman merchant today in the market."

Antonius was panting so hard that he was unable to answer. As he gasped for breath he noticed that he was near the entrance to the *amphitheatrum*. A few late spectators were rushing to their seats. The only other people in the square were a group of lounging Roman soldiers.

Just as Antonius was about to speak, the legionnaires leapt to attention. His captor did the same, while continuing to hold him firmly. He strained to see what was happening. A group of officials with their wives was being escorted into the square by another group of soldiers. Slaves carrying a large awning protected the dignitaries from the hot afternoon sun.

Antonius squinted. Then he began to shout. "Aurelius. Aurelius. It's me, Antonius!"

"Shut up, boy, or I'll have you whipped." The soldier's grip tightened until Antonius thought he would scream.

Then a familiar tall figure detached itself from the official party and strode over to them.

"Jupiter be praised," Aurelius exclaimed. "It is indeed the son of Fabius whom we had given up as dead. Are you all right?"

Antonius nodded through the pain and the soldier's grip relaxed. He had never been so happy to see anyone in his life as this quiet Roman official who had sailed with them from Ostia.

"Soldier," Aurelius commanded. "Run directly to the docks, to the ship known as the *Isis*, moored near the Antonine Baths. Inform the merchant Fabius that his son is safe and that he is with me at the games."

"Yes, sir," the soldier replied meekly.

Everything was happening so fast that Antonius felt dizzy. One moment he was lost in the back streets of Carthage, the next he was attending the games with dignitaries. He felt as if he was floating as he was escorted along with the governor of Carthage and his official party to the best seats in the *amphitheatrum*. He sat beside Aurelius who seemed less interested in what was happening on the field than in the conversation he was having with the governor's wife.

They sat down just as the trumpets sounded for the main event. The crowd cheered eagerly as the two combatants entered the ring, hoping for a good contest. One was a gladiator called the *retiarius*. He was armed with a trident, dagger and net. His opponent was the *secutor*, fully armed with a sword and shield. They would fight until one of them surrendered.

There was a hush throughout the arena as the fight began, the two gladiators circling each other slowly, jockeying for position. Suddenly the *retiarius* swung his net and threw it toward his enemy. If it landed truly, the *secutor* would be helpless. Instead it barely missed, catching for a second on the tip of his sword.

Gladiators in the Arena

Gladiators were usually slaves, prisoners of war or criminals. They were trained in schools, which were like prisons, where they were taught how to fight using different kinds of weapons and took part in gymnastic exercises to keep fit. When a gladiator won a fight, he was given money, and sometimes gladiators became so wealthy and famous that they were able to buy their freedom.

In addition to fights between armed gladiators, there were bloody matches between men and wild beasts **(above right)**. Perhaps cruellest of all were the spectacles in which an unarmed man was sent into the ring to face a hungry leopard or lion.

Huge arenas were built across the Empire for the games. The Colosseum in Rome could seat 50,000 people. It had underground chambers **(far right)**

where a gladiator waited his turn to fight, and where the wild beasts were kept in cages until a system of elevators brought them up to the level of the pit.

Great hunts were also staged in the arenas, and on one occasion 5,000 animals were killed. For these mock hunts, lions, tigers, leopards, panthers, bulls, hippopotamuses, rhinoceroses, bears and elephants were captured from all over the Empire and loaded onto ships bound for Rome.

The *retiarius* and the *secutor* in combat. The *retiarius* has thrown his net without managing to ensnare his enemy. Thrown off guard, he struggles against the *secutor* who remains well protected by a large shield.

Now the *retiarius* had only his trident and dagger. He broke into a run as the *secutor* gave chase, turning every few minutes, trying to jab his pursuer. But each thrust was skilfully blocked by the *secutor*'s shield. The crowd laughed and howled insults. It looked as though the *retiarius* was about to face a bloody end. The more he ran, the more he tired beneath the hot sun. Suddenly he lost his balance and fell to the ground. The crowd sprang to their feet. "Finish him off," some of them shouted. No one was laughing now. But somehow the *retiarius* summoned enough energy to roll out of the way of a fatal blow. As he did so, he scored a hit on the *secutor*'s leg. The crowd roared with approval.

As the *secutor* limped away, the *retiarius* raised one finger, begging mercy from the crowd. All over the arena the people raised their handkerchiefs and waved them madly in the air, cheering. The *retiarius* was a popular fighter. This time, at least, his life would be spared.

Antonius took a deep breath. He hated it at the Colosseum in Rome whenever a gladiator was killed. Sometimes he had a nightmare in which he was a *venator* being mauled by a lion. The dream always ended with his own blood staining the hard-packed dirt a dark red.

* * *

Antonius sat with a newly sharpened stylus and wax tablet, carefully noting each item of cargo as it was brought on board the *Isis*. This was the highest responsibility his father had ever given him—a clear sign that he had been forgiven for getting lost after chasing the thief. "Next time, think before you go dashing into a strange crowd in a strange city," his father had rebuked him. But he could tell his father was more relieved than angry. Even worse, Aunt Claudia had hugged him and kissed him as if he were a little boy.

Fabius had done well with the money Gildo had paid him for the wine. He had bought 500 amphoras of garum—chosen after carefully tasting several different kinds—1,000 sacks of grain, and fifty great slabs of beautiful yellow marble from the Numidian quarries of Chemtou that would fetch unbelievably high prices in Rome.

Once this heavy cargo was on board, including the 4,000 amphoras of olive oil that Aurelius had purchased, the slaves carried on bundles of ivory and ebony that had been brought over a caravan route from Leptis Magna. Then they brought on board crates of red household pottery—jars, lamps, cups, bowls—carefully chosen by Aunt Claudia. There was even a terracotta statue of Venus that she would offer to the goddess on Mount Eryx, where they would stop on the return trip to Ostia. Claudia had been particularly successful on her visit to the textile merchant, purchasing bright woven rugs, bolts of cloth, blankets and pillows. She had also bought beautiful gold earrings for his sister Julia and a necklace for his mother.

Loading the *Isis*

At the port in Carthage, slaves load the *Isis* with goods to be shipped to Rome.

1. Sacks of African grain.

2. Ivory and ebony from further inland in Africa.

3. Crates of red household pottery.

4. Slabs of yellow marble used to decorate cities and villas.

5. Amphoras full of olive oil and garum of the finest quality.

6. Bundles of woven rugs, cloth, pillows and blankets of intricate designs and rich hues.

7. A leopard in its iron cage, being shipped to Italy for the games.

Finally, the leopard was carried onto the deck and down into the hold, snarling and baring its teeth and clawing at its iron cage. This was his father's most exciting purchase. If they could get back to Rome before the Emperor's games, it would fetch as much money as five hundred jars of garum. The wild cat was the largest Antonius had ever seen, with beautiful markings and powerful limbs—he hoped the cage was a strong one. The leopard would be a dangerous adversary for the best of the gladiators.

The following day, after an uneventful voyage from Carthage under clear skies, the *Isis* arrived at the Sicilian port of Drepana. This was the moment the pilgrims had been waiting for, and they pushed and jostled one another to leave the ship so that they could reach the foot of Mount Eryx and climb to the Temple of Venus before sundown. The sailing master and the rest of the crew were left behind to keep an eye on the ship and its valuable cargo.

Antonius was in a good mood as he set off along the winding trail up the mountain. He had heard about the famous temple on Mount Eryx all his life, and could hardly wait to see it. Just ahead of him, his father, Aurelius and the captain were chatting amiably. Beside

him was his aunt, also in high spirits. Claudia's slave Syra walked behind them, carrying a jar of water in case they became thirsty.

As they walked, Claudia told Antonius about the many temples she had visited on her travels. "I have even been to the Temple of Isis in Alexandria," she told him. "She's the ancient goddess who watches over our ship."

As they climbed, the air became cooler and the sun dipped toward the horizon. Clouds hung near the summit, and it seemed to Antonius that he was climbing into the heavens themselves. As the path entered the clouds the pilgrims grew quiet. It was strange and somewhat scary to be walking in mist so high above the sea.

They emerged from the cloud onto the summit just as the rays of the setting sun were hitting the columns of the temple, bathing it in a golden light. Many people gasped. Some fell to the ground and offered a prayer on the spot to the goddess.

On the steps of the temple an old woman sat beside a large wooden cage full of doves, which she was selling for the sacrifice. Antonius held his dove tightly between his hands as he entered the cool silent temple. The sweet smell of burning incense filled his nostrils as the group of pilgrims from the *Isis* presented their offerings to the high priestess. But before she could complete the ceremony, one of the doves escaped, flying out between the columns of the temple, and the sacrifice was ruined. When this happened, Antonius noticed that his aunt turned white as a ghost. When they emerged into the twilight, Claudia was silent and frowning.

As the pilgrims began their slow descent by torchlight, a gloomy mood fell over the party. Those who were talking at all did so in hushed tones. Antonius stole away from his aunt and caught up with his father and the captain.

"Venus has always looked after seamen," the captain was saying, "and the spoiling of her sacrifice tells me there's a storm brewing. We'll have to sail back to Ostia along the coast."

"You are an old friend, but you are too timid," Fabius replied. "That will take many more days. The Emperor's games will be over and the leopard could die before the spring games begin."

"You may not see Rome again if we don't pay heed to Venus," replied the captain angrily.

Antonius remembered the conversation he'd overheard the night before their departure from Ostia.

"If you don't sail straight for Ostia as we agreed, I will refuse to pay your fee and I will never hire you again," Fabius replied, his own voice rising.

The captain said nothing more, and the two men continued down the mountain in a frosty silence.

* * *

Hard as he tried, there was nothing Antonius could do to cheer up Aunt Claudia. The sun was shining brightly, the *Isis* was clipping nicely through the sparkling blue water as it left Drepana, but she just sat unhappily on the deck, surrounded by her bundles of clothing and the gifts she had bought in the market in Carthage. She didn't even snap at Syra. She just stared into space.

Antonius left her to see what was happening at the stern. But he didn't stay there long. The captain barked

This Roman coin made in 57 B.C. shows the crowned head of Venus on one side and the Temple of Venus that stood on Mount Eryx on the other.

orders at anyone who crossed his path. Obviously Fabius had won their argument. Soon the coast of Sicily faded into the distance as the *Isis* headed out into the open water of the Tyrrhenian Sea. If all went well, they would be in Ostia the next day.

But before long the wind grew stronger and shifted to the northeast, making it impossible to hold the ship on course. The helmsman turned the bow away from the wind and the *Isis* headed even further from land, back toward Africa. Black clouds filled the sky and the day became dark.

"Lower the foresail, take in the topsail and reef the mainsail!" shouted the captain. Sailors immediately scurried up the rope ladders to reduce the amount of sail. Others tied down everything that could move and rigged rope lines for the passengers to hold onto if the sea got rougher.

As the waves and wind increased, it became more and more difficult to control the ship.

"I need relieving tackle," shouted the helmsman. The force of the wind made the strain on his arms unbearable. Quickly ropes and pulleys were rigged to help keep the tiller in place.

But the ship was becoming almost impossible to steer as it was tossed like a cork on the huge waves. Spray flew over the deck and the frightened passengers held on for dear life. Claudia was holding onto a rope with one hand while clutching her belongings with another.

Antonius, who was clinging tightly to the prow rail, ducked as a wave hit and salt water washed onto the deck.

Then the storm unleashed its full fury. The rain poured down, drenching the crew and passengers. Deafening claps of thunder were followed by great bolts of lightning that seemed to split the sky. Despite the roaring of the thunder, wind and waves, Antonius could hear the leopard's terrified screams from the hold of the ship. As the hours passed, the *Isis* was blown further and further off course.

Suddenly the *Isis* rose on a huge wave and then shot down the crest, nearly swamping itself. Several sailors were flung into the sea and the passengers screamed in terror. Antonius watched helplessly as his father attempted to throw floats to men who'd gone overboard, but the wind was too strong.

Then a second big wave crashed over the stern, sweeping the captain and the helmsman away with it. Fabius tried to reach the stern, but the ship now had a mind of its own as it pitched and heaved in the waves. Just as Fabius reached the tiller, Antonius saw another wave wash his father overboard.

People were throwing their belongings into the sea and jumping overboard as Antonius scrambled on his

hands and knees down the slippery, lurching deck toward Aunt Claudia and Syra. He reached the women just as the ship turned on its side and the three of them were tossed together into the churning water. Despite the wailing of the wind and the roaring of the sea, he thought he heard his aunt cry, "Isis! Save us! Isis!"

The next thing Antonius knew he was under water with no idea which way was up. His lungs were bursting as he swam frantically. Finally he reached the surface, swallowing mouthfuls of salt water as he gasped for air.

A large plank of wood from the ship banged into him and he grabbed on tightly.

In the next flash of lightning Antonius saw that the *Isis* was gone. Here and there people were bobbing in the water, clinging to pieces of wreckage or floating cargo, but there was no sign of his father and Aunt Claudia.

Suddenly he felt exhausted. The last thing he remembered before everything went black was thinking how angry his mother would be when he returned home in wet clothes.

CHAPTER SIX

The *Isis* Rediscovered · 1989

At 11 p.m. on Saturday, May 6, we wrapped up our last show from the Marsili Seamount and headed the ship back toward Skerki Bank and the *Isis* site. *Medea* and JASON had already proved their ability to make oceanography live for us in an amazing new way. Now they would have a chance to do the same for marine archaeology. Not only would we be able to get up close to the wreck, we would bring to the surface long-lost artifacts from the ancient world, the deepest objects ever recovered from a Roman wreck. What stories would they tell us of that distant time?

On board for this phase of our expedition was archaeologist Dr. Anna McCann, one of the pioneers of underwater archaeology and an expert on Roman trade and ancient artifacts. In the 1950s, not long after Jacques Cousteau invented the aqualung, Anna was one of the first archaeologists to go scuba diving on ancient wrecks. Anna would direct our investigation of the *Isis* and a nearby debris field we'd nicknamed Amphora Alley. She would make sure that the correct archaeological procedures were followed.

Joining her as head of our conservation team was Mary-Lou Florian, a conservation scientist from the Royal British Columbia Museum in Victoria, Canada. Mary-Lou's job was to make sure that any objects we brought up from the wreck would be preserved.

Anna hoped to come up with a rough date for the wreck, figure out what cargo the *Isis* was carrying and get some idea of what route the ship had followed and where she was heading. Each wreck that is excavated adds to our knowledge of life in the ancient world. So the *Isis* would provide one more piece of a puzzle being worked on by hundreds of scholars sifting evidence from other wreck sites and land excavations.

The most common clues a marine archaeologist has to work with are amphoras. Thousands of ancient amphoras have been recovered, and are now being classified and dated according to their shapes and stamps. Amphora types often last for one hundred years or more, so amphoras do not usually give us the precise date of a shipwreck. But by comparing what we found on the *Isis* with amphoras already studied, Anna hoped to be able to determine approximately when the ship sank and which ports she had stopped at on her journey. By analyzing the types of clay she might be able to identify where they were made and what they contained. Sometimes amphoras are found still corked and sealed with mortar. Recently archaeologists drank some wine that had been bottled 2,000 years ago. Not surprisingly, it had turned to vinegar. If we found corked amphoras we would definitely know what cargo the *Isis* was carrying.

As well as amphoras, an oil lamp could help us date the wreck as Roman oil lamps can be dated within fifty years of when they were made. If we found any wood

Students visiting the *Star Hercules* examine *Medea*, our new underwater camera sled.

from the hull we could determine its age through carbon-dating and tree-ring dating.

Archaeologists already know quite a lot about trade in Roman times. But the more we learn the better we can understand the conditions that helped Rome's rise and led to her decline and fall.

Where did the *Isis* wreck fit into the story of Rome? We hoped to find out soon.

Early on Sunday morning, May 7, we arrived at Skerki Bank and prepared for the day's first TV broadcast. We were eager to relocate the *Isis*—what a thrill it would be if we could find the wreck on live television! In bright sunshine and gentle seas we launched *Medea*, while JASON waited patiently on board. Once *Medea*'s cameras located the ship, JASON could go to work.

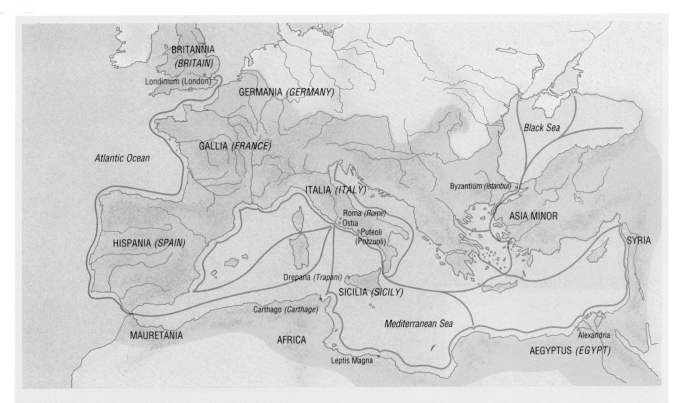

The Power of Rome

By the beginning of the third century B.C., Rome was an important city state, but it was not until she defeated the Carthaginian Empire, ruled by the city of Carthage in North Africa, that she became a big Mediterranean power. By the time of the birth of Christ, the first emperor Augustus ruled over almost all of the Mediterranean world. The Mediterranean was a Roman lake, and the main trade routes led to Rome.

The city of Rome at the height of the Empire was large even by modern standards — perhaps a million or more people. It included many of the richest families in the Empire and the poorest. The emperor kept the common people happy by controlling the price of grain and by offering free entertainments including circuses, or horse races. The most essential import was grain. Many years earlier, Rome had ceased growing enough to feed itself. Grain to make bread came from Egypt and North Africa; the wild animals for the games and circuses from Asia and Africa.

By the late third century A.D. the Roman Empire had grown to the point where it could no longer defend itself, and Rome was more dependent on food from North Africa than ever before. Eventually, in the late fourth century A.D., the Empire was split in two. The eastern half, ruled from Constantinople, survived for many centuries as the Byzantine Empire, but the western half was overrun by various warlike tribes.

(Above) This map shows the Roman Empire from the second to the fourth century A.D. The main sea trade routes and many ports are also indicated.
(Below) In this mosaic, sailors lead an antelope onto a ship bound for Rome.

By the third show of the day, we'd seen huge expanses of mud and quite a few isolated amphoras as we carefully worked our way back and forth over the target area — roughly six square miles (fifteen square kilometres) of bottom. This was the area we planned to explore in detail over the coming week. Betsey Robinson, who'd been on watch for the exciting first discovery of the *Isis* with my son Todd, was back at the data logging station, patiently recording every blip on the bottom revealed by *Medea*'s high-altitude black-and-white camera. We used this camera during every search because it showed us a bigger area of the sea floor than the other cameras. Louise Jones, a high school student on the expedition, was at *Medea*'s controls. This was her first chance to fly *Medea* and she was squeezing the joystick so hard I almost thought it would break.

I had barely finished my program introduction when the camera spotted a single amphora, and then another.

"I think we're coming in on the target," I said. Then a whole group of amphoras came into view. "We've got it! Bingo! Fantastic!" I yelled.

"The mother lode! We're here!" crowed Dana Yoerger, the navigator. "All right!"

Whoops, whistles and hollers filled the van as everyone temporarily forgot they were on live TV.

"You just saw how professional we are when we make our discoveries," I joked as the van team settled down. "I don't know where we are in the program, but I don't think it really matters."

A few minutes later, Anna McCann joined us, bursting with excitement at the prospect of getting her first

(Left) We carefully lower *Medea* over the side of the ship.
(Above) Shouts and cheers break out in the van when we relocate the *Isis*.

live look at the *Isis*. She didn't have to wait long. Now that we'd locked in on the wreck's position, we could easily return there. Using the *Star Hercules'* dynamic positioning system, Dana would be able to keep us hovering over the site.

As the group of amphoras again appeared on the screen, Anna was bubbling. "Just imagine, you are seeing what no one has seen for almost two thousand years," she told our audience. It was a startling thought. Who had those amphoras belonged to? Perhaps a Roman or North African merchant who'd set sail dangerously late in the season in the hope of making a good profit when others were afraid to take the risk?

Now, as we inspected the wreck site more carefully, we could see that it contained quite a variety of objects. The round object we'd spotted in 1988 was indeed a grindstone, and partly buried in the sediment was what looked like a large pot.

"We may be over the ship's galley," Anna guessed.

I felt relieved and happy. Now we could get on with our archaeological studies. Our first job was to carefully map the *Isis* site and the surrounding debris field under Anna's expert guidance. Before we lifted a single object, we wanted to have a complete visual record, so we would know exactly where each object came from. It was important to record this for future study and for the information of other visitors to the site. Then we would begin to raise our first artifacts from the ancient world.

Anna McCann and a crew member study maps of the wreck site **(inset)** as JASON explores below.

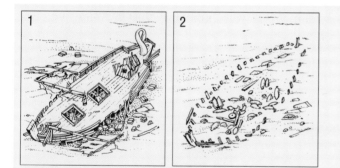

What happens to a ship after it sinks?

1. This picture shows the remains of the *Isis* and its cargo right after sinking.

2. One thousand years later, the leopard, the sails, ropes, cloth goods, sacks of grain, and much of the wood of the ship have disappeared, devoured by marine organisms. Other substances have decomposed more slowly.

3. More than 1,600 years later, very little wood remains, although much more may lie buried beneath the sediment where there are fewer wood-eating marine organisms. Possibly large slabs of marble, ivory and ebony lie beneath the sediment too. The grindstone has survived. Many amphoras and some of the everyday pottery are still intact, although some pieces have been broken by the movement of the seawater or sediment. Corals and other sea life have found a home by clinging to the surface of the pottery.

3 The *Isis* wreck site

1. Amphora—Africana Grande
2. Amphora—Africana Piccolo
3. Remains of metal with wood from ship.
4. Grindstone
5. Metal remains—possibly part of an iron cage, a grill from a stove or an iron anchor.
6. Pot
7. Cup
8. Flat-bottomed amphora
9. Small amphora—may have stood in a tripod and held wine.
10. Jug—possibly for garum.
11. Small oil lamp
12. Two-handled jug

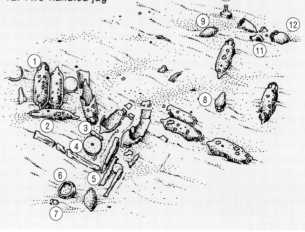

CHAPTER SEVEN

Exploring the *Isis* Wreck

By Monday our mapping of the *Isis* wreck site and the debris field was complete. We were ready for JASON to go to work. This was a moment we'd all been waiting for, but there were a number of questions hanging over us. Would JASON be able to lift the amphoras and other objects without damaging them? What would happen to pottery that had been submerged for centuries if it was suddenly brought back to the surface? One expert had warned us that the amphoras would fall apart when we took them out of the water. No archaeologist had ever brought up an amphora from this depth before. We were about to enter the unknown.

For this delicate operation, JASON's mechanical arm was fitted with a pair of curved tongs. These tongs,

nicknamed "Knuckles," were designed to grasp an amphora without damaging it. Attached to the lower set of tongs was some soft netting that formed the "scoop bag," which would cradle each amphora.

Team members crowded into the control van as we began the recovery of our first amphora. First Anna, Mary-Lou and Martin Bowen, at JASON's controls, decided which amphoras to excavate. Those selected

We dropped our elevator, loaded with a steel weight, over the side of the ship a safe distance away from the wreck site. Once JASON had filled the elevator's net compartments with artifacts, we sent an acoustic command pulsing through the water to a transponder on the elevator. This caused the elevator to release its weight and rise to the surface with the help of three glass floats.

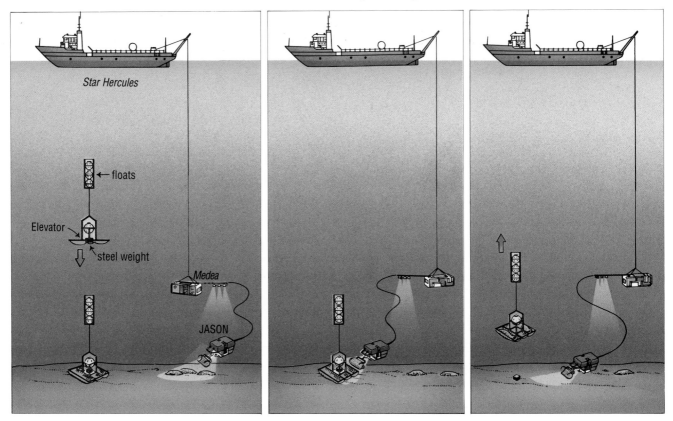

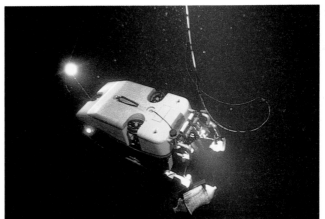

had to be whole, or not badly cracked, and of a size that JASON could grasp. They also had to be in a position where JASON could retrieve them without harming other artifacts.

Martin was determined to show his audience what the robot could do. We held our breath as he brought JASON ever so slowly toward the target, one of the large North African jars that had carried the *Isis*'s cargo. It was hard to believe all this was taking place 2,684 feet (818 metres) down; it seemed as close as the next room.

Now came the tricky part. We all watched tensely as Martin gently worked the scoop bag into the soft sediment beneath the jar. At last, with a decisive plop, the huge amphora settled into the net without a scratch. As Knuckles gently closed around the jar, we sighed with relief.

"That was one giant grab for mankind," joked Mary-Lou as cheers and applause erupted in the van.

But Martin's job wasn't over yet. A short distance away from JASON was our elevator, a device made out of pipes and soft fish netting that would carry the artifacts to the surface. Soon the elevator loomed into view on JASON's forward camera. Martin approached cautiously. He didn't want to make any mistakes now. Finally, with the amphora poised just above one of the elevator's net compartments, he opened the tongs and placed the jar gently in its berth.

After a couple of hours' work, each compartment of the elevator contained an amphora. Now these ancient jars would have to pass their next test. By the time the elevator reached the surface of the water fifteen minutes later, a crowd was out on deck.

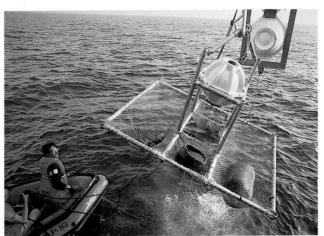

(Above left) Skip Gleason built the elevator which would allow us to retrieve objects from the deep sea. Here he holds "Knuckles," the tongs which JASON will use to pick up amphoras on the sea floor.

(Top) JASON clutches an amphora with Knuckles.

(Middle) JASON slowly moves toward the underwater elevator with his precious cargo.

(Above) The elevator breaks the surface of the water, bringing a huge amphora and a large pot from the shipwreck in its net compartments. The Zodiac will tow the elevator over to the *Star Hercules*.

It was almost impossible to believe that these long, elegant but sturdy-looking pottery containers, dripping with seawater and glistening in the warm sun, had been lost for so long. After they'd been hoisted on board and carefully submerged in the "swimming pool" we'd built for the conservation team, I walked over and ran my hand over the surface of one of the big jars. Parts were covered with marine growths and beautiful pink corals, but where the pottery was bare it was still smooth and shiny, as if it had come fresh from the kiln. Whose was the last hand to touch this, I wondered. A slave who'd loaded the jars in Carthage? The captain of the *Isis*, examining his cargo to make sure it was stowed securely for the rapidly approaching storm? The merchant who'd risked taking one last voyage so late in the sailing season? Or perhaps his son, along for the excitement of his first sea voyage and exploring below decks when the captain wasn't looking?

It was like something out of a time machine. I was face to face with the world of ancient Rome, a world I'd only read about in history books. Now I was touching objects from that world with my own hand. Suddenly the story of the *Isis* no longer seemed like a daydream, but a flesh-and-blood reality.

As the days passed, I watched as pieces of this ancient puzzle—the *Isis*—were brought to the surface. Each artifact was examined in minute detail. What had it been used for? What had it contained? How old was it? What part of the ship had it come from? Gradually some of the pieces of the puzzle began to fall into place.

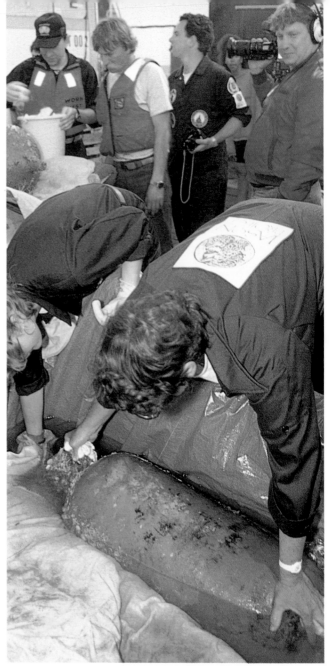

(Above left) The first load of artifacts arrives on deck.
(Above) An ancient amphora is placed in the "swimming pool" to prevent it from cracking.

Anna had no doubt now that the *Isis* was a cargo ship. She also knew that the types of amphoras the *Isis* was carrying were from the late Roman period of the third and fourth centuries A.D. That meant our wreck was one of a very few ships ever discovered from this period.

The *Isis* was carrying two kinds of late Roman amphoras known as "Africana Piccolo" and "Africana Grande" (literally "little African" and "big African"). Since both were made in Tunisia, Anna was confident the ship was coming from an African port—perhaps

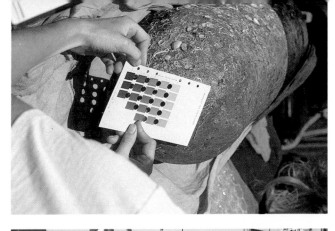

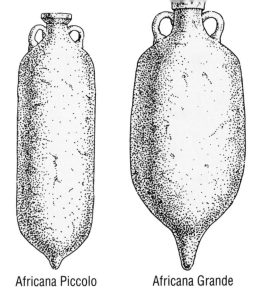

Africana Piccolo   Africana Grande

(Above left) This chart helps archaeologists record the precise shade of the ceramic.

(Left) We measure one of the Africana Grande amphoras.

(Above) Amphoras of the Africana Piccolo type were used mainly for fish sauce or garum. The Africana Grande type could hold 18 gallons (68 litres) of olive oil.

(Below) This wall painting from Pompeii shows cupids sampling wine from amphoras similar to those we raised from Amphora Alley.

Carthage — because when a cargo ship reached its destination, amphoras were emptied and discarded. And since both of these types have been found at Ostia, Rome's seaport town, it seemed logical that the ship was sailing from the North African port of Carthage to Rome.

But we'll never be sure exactly what cargo was on board. None of the amphoras we brought up from the *Isis* was still sealed, so we can only guess at their contents. Almost all evidence of other types of cargo would have disappeared soon after the ship sank.

Since we didn't have the equipment to excavate below the surface, or scan with sonar, Anna could only guess at the size of the ship. But from the amount and type of material we could see, in what appeared to be the galley, she speculated that the *Isis* could have been a good-sized Roman merchant ship of this period. It might have been around 200 tons and carried as many as 5,000 amphoras. So thousands of amphoras may still be sitting stacked in neat rows hidden beneath the bottom sediment. And perhaps large sections of the wooden hull are still preserved.

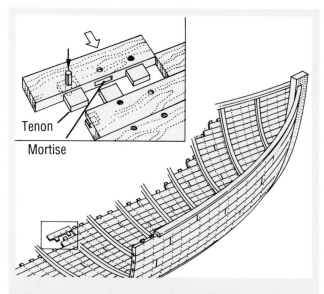

Tenon

Mortise

Building an Ancient Ship

When constructing a ship, a Roman shipbuilder started with the planking, which he carefully joined by rows of mortises and tenons. He then inserted the frame into the hull. Archaeologists call this the "shell-first" method — in contrast to the "frame-first" technique that is used today. In the "frame-first" method, the shipbuilder starts with the skeleton or frame and then adds the planking.

The piece of wood we brought up showing the mortise and tenon system of shipbuilding was later identified as white oak, which grows in Europe and Italy, but not in North Africa. So the *Isis* must have been built in Italy.

We did bring up a piece of wood that must have come from the hull because it showed part of a mortise and tenon joint typical of ancient shipbuilding. We also saw what looked like some lead sheathing. With the close-up camera system even the tiny rivets could be seen clearly. Ancient ships' hulls were often covered with lead or copper sheathing.

So we knew for sure that we had a merchant ship, that it was likely coming from Carthage and heading for Ostia. And we had strong evidence to date it within a two-hundred-year period from the third to the fourth centuries A.D.

Anna's detective work became more difficult when she examined the other *Isis* artifacts we brought up to the surface. These were bits and pieces from the daily life of those who had been on board, objects that would have been used during the voyage — some of them moments before the ship plunged to the bottom.

What was the function of the pot? When we brought it to the surface we found that it contained a hardened material that looked like resin and had a large, flattish stone embedded in it. The outside of the pot was blackened — probably it had been heated over a fire in the galley. Had it contained pine resin used to seal the cracks in the hull timbers? Was the stone a tool for applying the heated resin, or had it fallen into the pot during the ship's descent? Perhaps one of the crewmen had been slaving over the deck when the captain ordered him to hurry to help reduce the sail before the storm hit.

The variety of amphora shapes as well as table pottery we raised supported Anna's original guess that the area of the wreck we could see might be the ship's galley. The round grindstone might have been used by the galley slave to grind spices or flour for bread. There was a pottery cup as well as several smaller amphoras and pitchers.

Perhaps the merchant or his son had poured wine from that pitcher and drunk from the cup during the last meal of their ill-fated journey. These everyday things made the wreck seem like something that had just happened to people like us, not something that had taken place over 1,600 years ago.

Some of the mysteries that remain may be solved by further scientific analysis. The pot will be X-rayed to see if anything is buried in the resin. The resin itself can be carbon-dated. Analysis of the pottery may reveal where each amphora or other clay vessel was made — if Anna can match the type of clay used with clay beds that we know were used by the Romans.

It was not until our final day on site that we recovered the most exciting object for Anna — a Roman lamp. Perhaps this lamp, filled with olive oil, provided a flicker of light in the dark galley of the *Isis*. Lamps can be dated much more closely than amphoras or other pottery, so this was an especially lucky find. After comparing its shape, decoration and type of clay with other Roman lamps, Anna was able to say with reasonable confidence that the ship, coming from North Africa, went down in the second half of the fourth century A.D.

(Top) Louise Jones keeps a stream of water flowing over a small jug that was probably used at a table to hold garum.

(Left) When the small oil lamp was dry we were able to see that the nozzle of the lamp had been blackened by burning oil.

(Middle) This amphora is covered with tiny sea corals and marine growths.

(Right) Although over 1,600 years old, this cup is similar to pottery cups made today.

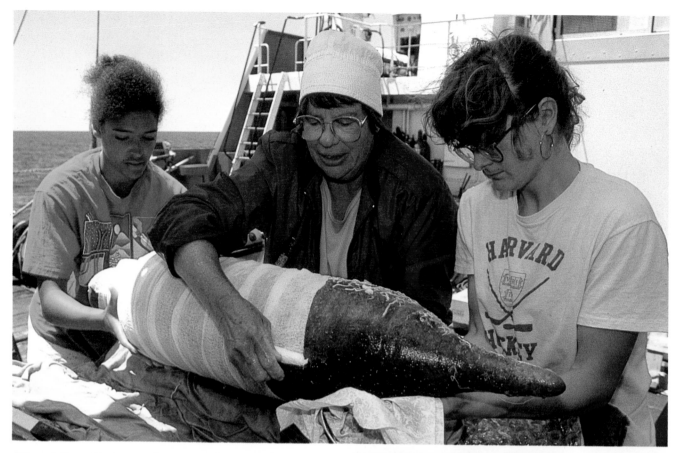

(Above) The artifacts were first wrapped in sterile bandages soaked in water, to prevent tiny fungi from growing on them. Then they were wrapped in water-soaked gauze to make sure the bandages stayed wet, and covered in plastic wrap to keep the moisture in. The next layer was tin foil and, finally, layers of bubble pack were wrapped around the foil to prevent damage from bumps.

(Right) Inside the pot we found some iron nails, a piece of wood and what may be a piece of string or leather.

During the two weeks we spent exploring the *Isis* and nearby Amphora Alley, we raised forty-two objects from the ancient world. These objects were selected from the many sighted by *Medea* and JASON.

As each was brought to the surface on our trusty elevator, it went through a rigorous scientific process requiring close teamwork between Anna McCann and Mary-Lou Florian, in charge of conservation. Once the archaeologist had examined each object, Mary-Lou took over. Her job was to make sure that these precious remnants of a lost civilization would survive intact for further study and eventual display in a museum.

Conservators work hand in hand with archaeologists at all times. But their job is especially important in marine archaeology where the artifacts have become saturated with salt water. If you simply brought an amphora to the surface and let it dry out, the salt that had worked its way into the pottery would crystallize and may cause the jar to crack. So the first step in the conservation of these objects is to keep them wet. That's why we had built the small swimming pool. That pool was the first stop for everything we brought on board.

The next step was to package the amphoras for transport all the way back to Woods Hole, Massachusetts, and still keep them wet. Pottery objects are usually left in salt water for transport, because

(Above) A selection of the ancient artifacts from the *Isis* are now ready to be displayed in a museum.

ceramic can sometimes crack if it is transferred directly from salt water to fresh water. But Mary-Lou wanted to use fresh water to prevent marine fungi and bacteria from deteriorating the packing materials. She discussed this problem with a geologist on board. Because of the nature of the clay material, they decided this cracking would not occur, and that it would be all right to use fresh water for storing and packaging. So Mary-Lou packaged some of the amphoras in fresh water.

Several weeks later, when Mary-Lou unwrapped the amphoras at Woods Hole, she discovered that the ones wrapped and stored in fresh water were in better shape than the ones in salt water. The wet bandages had caused the salts to come out much faster. This discovery will undoubtedly influence future conservation of objects recovered from the deep sea. Once the salts have been completely removed, and the amphoras and other objects are dry, they will be carefully studied for any additional clues they can give us about the fate of the *Isis*.

EPILOGUE

When the last amphora had been wrapped up like an Egyptian mummy, and the *Star Hercules* headed toward Sicily, I knew that the JASON Project was finally drawing to a close — at least for this year. On our way home we hoped to find one of the greatest battleships of World War II, the *Bismarck*. But already I felt proud that we had accomplished so much against so many odds. We'd survived near catastrophe with the loss of JASON and *Hugo*. We'd taken untested technology and put it to work. And we'd involved 250,000 students in oceanography and archaeology during live broadcasts from the bottom of the Mediterranean Sea.

With this success under our belts we are ready to take on exciting new challenges. In the coming years, using JASON and *Argo*, we plan to explore the Great Lakes, looking at wrecks from the War of 1812. And I'd love to return to the *Titanic* to do live broadcasts from that grand old lady of the deep — and maybe unlock even more of her secrets. Perhaps we will return to the Mediterranean with the technology to actually excavate the *Isis* wreck and find out what lies beneath the surface. And there are countless other ancient underwater sites to explore. Maybe we can find one of the sunken cities archaeologists believe lie off the coast of Sicily, or the remains of the battle of Salamis in 480 B.C., when the Greeks defeated their enemies the Persians and saved the city of Athens.

With JASON we will be able to explore the earth's last frontier, the deep ocean, ninety-eight percent of which has never been seen by human eyes. We will be able to find downed airplanes and lost submarines, inspect underwater pipelines and cables, and search for deep ocean mineral deposits. The archaeologist will be able to look and learn about the past without destroying it. And the miracle of telepresence means that a team of experts or interested onlookers can follow JASON without ever leaving land. Perhaps some day a robot descendant of JASON will explore beyond our galaxy.

But it is hard to believe that anything can be more exciting than our 1989 exploration of the *Isis*, and our brush with the story of a ship sailing from Carthage to Rome over 1,600 years ago. I hadn't expected the ship to come so alive in my imagination. As we explored the *Isis* wreck and brought the amphoras to the surface, I became aware of how little separates us from the ancient Romans. They breathed the same air, felt the same wind and sailed the same waters. Their lives were different and simpler in some ways, but they had many of the same hopes and fears.

As our ship steamed toward Sicily my thoughts shifted to the people who had sailed on the last voyage of the *Isis*. Had they all perished when the ship went down? Or did some live to tell their children and grandchildren the story of a great storm, the loss of a fine ship and her valuable cargo, and a miraculous rescue?

* * *

When Antonius opened his eyes, the early morning sun was shining on his face and the sea was calm. His body was chilled, locked in position around a plank of wood from the ship. When he tried to move he felt a shooting pain in one arm. He looked around in disbelief. Was this the underworld, the land of the dead? And then, not far away he spied Aunt Claudia clinging to a large plank. Gritting his teeth, he kicked and paddled his way over to her.

Trapped in Time: The Return of an Ancient Coin

When the resin in the bottom of the pot **(right)** was X-rayed, it revealed a round metal object. Could it possibly be a coin, Anna wondered.

To remove the "coin" a conservator carefully cored into the resin using the sharpened end of a heated brass pipe **(far right)**. When close to the coin, he used a brush and acetone to dissove the remaining resin, and finally removed a thin disk covered with corrosion.

Experts soon identified it as a *centenionalis*, a Roman bronze coin like a penny. Constantius II, the son of the Emperor Constantine appears on one side. The other side shows the Emperor spearing a fallen horseman. Here the Latin writing reads FEL TEMP REPARATIO promising a "happy renewal of the times," or even "happy days are here again." This coin and an identical coin in better condition are shown **(right)**.

The coin was probably minted around A.D. 355 which confirms that the *Isis* sank in the second half of the fourth century A.D. Who did this coin belong to? That remains a mystery.

"Antonius! Thank the gods you are alive. I haven't seen any of the others yet," said Aunt Claudia with a tremor in her voice. Her eyes filled with tears, but she quickly pulled herself together. "There's not much we can do but wait and hope."

Antonius' throat ached with thirst and he felt a dull pounding in his head. Aunt Claudia kept talking to him, trying to be cheerful, trying to keep him awake. But he fell into a dazed dreamlike state. Hours later he raised his head. Suddenly Aunt Claudia started shouting and waving.

"Antonius, look!" she exclaimed. He followed her finger, squinting to see with the sun in his eyes. In the distance he saw a small ship. Was it a pirate ship? He couldn't see the sail well enough to tell. A flash of fear went through him, but he was too exhausted to worry for long. Pirate ship or not, they needed any help they could get. Summoning all his strength, Antonius joined Claudia, shouting at the top of his lungs. They shouted until they were hoarse, and finally the ship headed toward them, looming larger and larger over the surface of the water. Sailors threw ropes out to them and they grasped on with trembling hands. First Claudia, then Antonius was hauled on board. The captain of the ship, a kind Carthaginian, gave them blankets and helped Claudia find a place to rest. But Antonius stood near the prow for a long time, staring out at the calm and empty blue sea.

GLOSSARY

A.D.: Anno Domini refers to the new era which began with the birth of Jesus Christ.

afterdeck: The part of the deck toward the rear end of a ship.

altimeter: An instrument that measures height above sea level.

aluminum (also spelled aluminium): a light, pliable metal.

amidships: The middle of a ship.

amphitheatrum: An oval or circular building with seats that rise in tiers around an open space where the games were put on.

amphora: A large round clay jar with two handles and usually a pointed "toe" or bottom, used for shipping or storage.

aqualung: A breathing apparatus used by divers with tanks of compressed air that are strapped to the back and feed air through a hose to the diver's mouth.

archaeology: The scientific study of people from the past and their cultures.

Argo: A steel sled equipped with sonar and video cameras that take moving television pictures. The pictures are transmitted via the sled's towing cable to the surface as *Argo* is pulled along 10 to 30 feet (3 to 10 metres) above the ocean floor.

artifact: An object, usually handmade, representing a group or culture.

basilica: A type of early Christian church.

B.C.: Before Christ.

Berbers: The original settlers of Tunisia, the Berbers were semi-nomads who lived off their herds of livestock.

bow: The front end of a ship.

caldarium: The hot baths in a Roman bath building.

carbon dating: A method of dating an organic or living archaeological material by measuring the decay of a chemical element called carbon 14 in it.

centurion: The commander in charge of a century, or one hundred men, in the Roman army.

conservator: A person who cares for and preserves artifacts.

coordinates: The numbers of latitude and longitude on a chart or map used to locate a particular point.

corrosion: The wearing away of metal through chemical action.

debris field: The area where objects from a shipwreck have fallen.

dynamic positioning: The technology that allows a ship to remain in a precise spot.

fantail: A fan-shaped overhang at the rear end of a ship.

fiber-optic cable (also spelled fibre-optic): A bundle of thin, flexible strands of glass which transmit light. A fiber-optic cable sends signals carrying video images from JASON and *Medea* to the research ship. The cable also contained copper wires which transmit power to the attached vehicles.

frigidarium: The cold baths in a Roman bath building.

garum: A fermented fish sauce eaten by the Romans.

geology: The scientific study of the earth and its rocks.

hold: The area below the decks of a ship where the cargo is stored.

Hugo *(Huge Argo)*: A sled, towed by the research ship, that hovers over the sea floor and provides a garage for JASON. *Hugo* surveys wide areas of the sea floor with side-scanning sonar and video cameras. Pictures are transmitted via the sled's towing cable to the surface.

hull: The frame or body of a ship without its superstructure.

hydrothermal vent: An opening in the sea floor through which cold water passes, and then comes out superheated by the hot liquid rock beneath the earth's crust.

hypocaust: A floor in a Roman bath raised on small columns of bricks to allow hot air to circulate underneath.

Isis (pronounced *ICE-es*): Egyptian mother goddess and patron goddess of sailors who promised an afterlife to believers.

JASON: A remotely-operated vehicle equipped with still and video cameras, JASON is capable of close inspection of the sea floor. Signals carrying the video images that JASON sees are transmitted to a camera sled and up to the ship through fiber-optic cables. JASON also has a robotic arm for gathering specimens.

Jupiter: King of the gods. He was called Zeus by the Greeks.

knot: The measure of a ship's speed equivalent to one nautical mile per hour.

lava: Hot liquid rock or magma that flows out onto the earth's surface.

leeward: On the sheltered side of a ship, away from the wind.

legionnaire: A member of a legion, a unit of 3,000 to 6,000 soldiers and cavalry in the Roman army.

magma: Molten rock material that moves within the earth.

Medea: A back-up sled that "flies" over the sea floor while being towed by a research ship. First used to test the fiber-optic cable, *Medea* was later adapted to replace *Hugo*.

molten: Made liquid by heat.

mortise: A hollow square notch cut out of a plank for a tenon to fit into.

mosaic: A picture or pattern made by joining together small pieces of stone or glass.

Neptune: The Roman god of the sea. He was called Poseidon by the Greeks.

ninepins: A game, similar to bowling, in which nine pins are knocked down with a ball.

nummus: A small Roman copper coin, like a penny. There were between 10,000 and 14,000 *nummi* to a gold coin called a *solidus*.

oceanography: The science of the ocean.

Phoenicians: The sea-trading people from ancient Phoenicia (now part of Lebanon) who settled many cities throughout the Mediterranean world including Carthage.

pilgrim: A person who travels to a holy place to worship.

plate tectonics: The theory that the earth's crust is made up of moving plates.

port: The left-hand side of a ship when facing forward.

propulsion: The force that drives or pushes an object forward.

prow: The pointed front part of a ship.

relief: A picture carved into a stone surface.

resin: A sticky inflammable substance that does not dissolve in water and comes from trees.

retiarius: A gladiator armed with a net, trident and dagger. Also called a net man.

rivets: Pins or bolts of metal that hold metal plates together.

rogue wave: A huge wave that can rise up suddenly causing great damage to ships at sea.

Saint Cyprian: A Christian bishop of Carthage who died for his faith in A.D. 258.

scuba: Self-contained underwater breathing apparatus.

seamount: An underwater mountain.

secutor: A gladiator who carries a sword and shield.

sediment: The silt which settles to the bottom of the ocean.

Serapis: An Egyptian god of the underworld, afterlife and fertility. Most Roman cities had a temple to Serapis, called a *Serapeum*.

skiff: A small sail boat or row boat.

sonar: A system used to detect and locate underwater objects by reflected sound waves.

starboard: The right-hand side of a ship when facing forward.

stem: The bow or prow of a ship.

stern: The rear end of a ship.

strigil: A scraper used by the Romans to remove oil, perspiration and dirt from the body.

stylus: A thin metal instrument with a hard, sharp point used for writing on clay or wax tablets in ancient times.

telepresence: The use of telecommunications to create a simulated presence at a remote site.

tenon: A square notch projecting from the side of a plank which fits into a mortise.

thruster: An engine that propels a vehicle.

transponder: A sonar device that receives a signal and then transmits its own signal. It is used as an underwater beacon to guide ships and vehicles.

trawler: A person or boat that fishes using a large net that drags along the ocean floor.

tree-ring dating: A method of dating through study of yearly growth rings in wood.

trident: A spear with three prongs.

tripod: A stand with three legs often used to support an amphora.

uplink: A signal sent up to a satellite from the earth.

venator: An armed man trained to fight a wild beast.

Venus: Roman goddess of love, fertility, the sea and sailors. She was called Aphrodite by the Greeks.

yard: A pole that hangs horizontally across a mast to support a square sail.

Zodiac: An inflatable rubber boat.

RECOMMENDED FURTHER READING

Exploring the Titanic
by Robert D. Ballard 1988
(Scholastic Inc., U.S./Pyramid, Octopus Books, U.K./Ashton Scholastic, Australia/Penguin Books, Canada)
The fascinating real-life adventure story of Robert Ballard's discovery of the *Titanic*.

The Discovery of the Titanic
by Robert D. Ballard 1987
(Warner, U.S./Hodder & Stoughton, U.K./Penguin Books, Canada)
An in-depth account of Robert Ballard's two *Titanic* expeditions with many photographs.

Diving to the Past, Recovering Ancient Wrecks
by W. John Hackwell 1988
(Charles Scribner's Sons)
Describes in words and pictures how ancient ships are salvaged and what they tell us about the past.

Exploring the Sea
by Carvel Blair 1986
(Random House Ltd.)
A fully-illustrated introduction to oceanography.

The Roman World
by Mike Corbishley 1986
(Franklin Watts Inc. U.S./Kingfisher Books, U.K.)
The history of Rome, the ancient Romans and how they lived, with many photographs, illustrations and maps.

Treasures of the Deep
by Walter Oleksy 1984
(Julian Messner, N.Y.)
Describes underwater expeditions in search of past civilizations, unusual sea creatures and sunken treasure ships.

JASON PARTNERS

Woods Hole Oceanographic Institution
The Quest Group Limited
Electronic Data Systems Corporation
National Geographic Society
The JASON Museum Network
National Science Foundation
Turner Broadcasting System, Inc.
National Science Teachers Association
The development of the ARGO/JASON system is funded by the U.S. Navy.

JASON MUSEUM NETWORK

Boston Museum of Science (Boston, MA)
Discovery Place (Charlotte, NC)
Museum of Science and Industry (Chicago, IL)
The Science Place (Dallas, TX)
Denver Museum of Natural History (Denver, CO)
Detroit Science Center (Detroit, MI)
Memphis Pink Palace Museum (Memphis, TN)
The Franklin Institute (Philadelphia, PA)
Rochester Museum and Science Center (Rochester, NY)
Mote Marine Laboratory (Sarasota, FL)
National Geographic Society Grosvenor Auditorium (Washington D.C.)
Royal British Columbia Museum (Victoria, British Columbia, Canada)

PICTURE CREDITS

Front Cover: (Top) Painting by Ken Marschall (Left) George F. Mobley © National Geographic Society (Middle and right) Joseph H. Bailey © National Geographic Society

Back Cover: (Top) Painting by Ken Marschall (Bottom) Quest Group Ltd.

Back Flap: George F. Mobley © National Geographic Society

Poster: (Left and middle) Paintings by Ken Marschall (Right) Quest Group Ltd.

Page 1: C M Dixon

2–3: Joseph H. Bailey © National Geographic Society

6–7: Painting by Ken Marschall

8–9: Quest Group Ltd.

10: George F. Mobley © National Geographic Society

11: (Top) © Jonathan Blair/Woodfin Camp and Associates (Inset) Emory Kristof © National Geographic Society (Bottom) Metropolitan Museum of Art, Harris Brisbane Dick Fund, 1934.

12–13: Illustration by Jack McMaster/Margo Stahl

13: George F. Mobley © National Geographic Society

14: (Top) Illustration by Jack McMaster/Margo Stahl (Left and right) George F. Mobley © National Geographic Society

15: George F. Mobley © National Geographic Society

16–17: George F. Mobley © National Geographic Society

18: (Top) Quest Group Ltd. (Left) George F. Mobley © National Geographic Society

19: Scala/Art Resource, N.Y.

20: C M Dixon

21: (Left) Courtesy of Anna Marguerite McCann (Right) Painting by Wes Lowe

22: Painting by Wes Lowe

23: Painting by Wes Lowe

24: The NY Carlsberg Glyptotek, Copenhagen

25: Painting by Wes Lowe

26: Thomas Kleindinst/Woods Hole Oceanographic Institution

27: (Top left) Courtesy of EDS Corporation (Bottom left and right) Joseph H. Bailey © National Geographic Society

28: (Left) Joseph H. Bailey © National Geographic Society (Right) Illustration by Jack McMaster/Margo Stahl

29: Joseph H. Bailey © National Geographic Society

30–31: Joseph H. Bailey © National Geographic Society

32: Joseph H. Bailey © National Geographic Society

33: Quest Group Ltd.

34: Illustration by Jack McMaster/Margo Stahl (Right) Joseph H. Bailey © National Geographic Society

35: (Left) Joseph H. Bailey © National Geographic Society (Top right) Thomas Kleindinst/Woods Hole Oceanographic Institution (Bottom right) Royal British Columbia Museum

36: Scala/Art Resource, N.Y.

37: Painting by Wes Lowe

39: Painting by Wes Lowe

40: (Left) Scala/Art Resource, N.Y. (Right) Nimatallah/Art Resource, N.Y.

41: Painting by Wes Lowe

42–43: Painting by Wes Lowe

44: Painting by Wes Lowe

45: Reproduced by Courtesy of the Trustees of the British Museum

46–47: Painting by Ken Marschall

48: Joseph H. Bailey © National Geographic Society

49: Illustration by Jack McMaster/Margo Stahl (Bottom) Sonia Halliday Photographs, Weston Turville

50: Joseph H. Bailey © National Geographic Society

51: (Top) Quest Group Ltd. (Inset) Joseph H. Bailey © National Geographic Society (Bottom) Illustration by Jack McMaster/Margo Stahl

52: Illustration by Jack McMaster/Margo Stahl

53: (Top left) Joseph H. Bailey © National Geographic Society (Top and middle right) Quest Group Ltd. (Bottom right) Joseph H. Bailey © National Geographic Society

54: Joseph H. Bailey © National Geographic Society

55: (Top and middle left) Joseph H. Bailey © National Geographic Society (Top right) Illustration by Jack McMaster/Margo Stahl (Bottom) Courtesy of Anne Laidlaw

56: Illustration by Jack McMaster/Margo Stahl

57: Joseph H. Bailey © National Geographic Society

58: Joseph H. Bailey © National Geographic Society

59: Thomas Kleindinst and John Porteous/Woods Hole Oceanographic Institution

61: (Top Left) Joseph H. Bailey © National Geographic Society (Top right) Courtesy of Dennis Piechota (Middle left and right) Courtesy of the American Numismatic Society (Bottom) Painting by Wes Lowe

Madison Press Books would like to thank the following people for their assistance and advice: Lionel Casson, Dennis Piechota, Betsey Robinson, Jennifer Blair of EDS Corporation, Cathy Offinger of the JASON Foundation for Education, Bill Allen, Lisa Page, Peter Schnall and Chris Weber of the National Geographic Society, Mary-Lou Florian of the Royal British Columbia Museum, Jonathan Wickham, Roger Torda and Lorraine Glynn of Turner Broadcasting System Inc., and Andy Bowen, Bill Lange, Gretchen McManamin and Rose Petrecca of Woods Hole Oceanographic Institution.